THE NIGHT I

WITH ROMMEL

by

Elisabeth Marrion

ISBN: 978-1-291-28112-5

This book is a historical novel based upon a true story, in certain parts, incidents or names have been added or changed.

PublishNation|London

For Moe

My best friend. Without her encouragement, this story would have never been told.

A big THANK YOU to my husband David and my daughter in law Jean,

just because ....

Grateful acknowledgement is made to :

Herr Wolfgang Stierle, Bezirksvorsteher (District Mayor), Stuttgart-Botnang (Germany)

Prologue

'Why do people die, Mamma?' I went over to where he stood and put my arms around him. Klaus pushed me away. 'The man Pappa works for, has he really died?'

How could I explain the horror of it all to a seven year old boy, but I could not lie to him.

'Yes, I think the man your Pappa works for, the Field Marshal, he is dead.

'But why, Mamma? Why do people die?'

'I think sometimes God wants them to come and live with him.' I hoped this would help him to understand.

'But doesn't God want everybody to come and live with him?'

'Yes he does, but special people, he might want those to live with him earlier and that is when God has to make a quick decision, you see?'

'You mean, like when he wanted Inge to come and live with him, even though we wanted Inge to stay here with us?'

'Yes Klaus, just like it was with Inge.' I had to look away, I did not want him to realise how hard it was not to cry.

'But my Pappa, my Pappa he will come home,' he said and went back into the kitchen to join the other children.

1

14th October 1944
Lunchtime
Herrlingen, Germany

They walked side by side, heads bent down, the two men speaking quietly. They took their time and went ahead towards the small woodland at the top of the hill, General Burgdorf to his left. Field Marshal Rommel now did most of the talking, holding his Field Marshal's baton tightly under his left arm. Occasionally the baton touched General Burgdorf's uniform when the Field Marshal turned to him whilst speaking.

Both men gathered speed now, their strides increasing in length, as if they just remembered there was an appointment to be kept and they did not dare to arrive late.

The dark green car, which drove them there, was standing in the open space at the edge of the forest. They assumed General Maisel and the driver were still inside.

General Burgdorf had ignored orders for the second time today. Firstly, just after breakfast, when the dark green car he travelled in, parked outside the Field Marshal's house and, in direct defiance of his orders, he told General Maisel and the driver to stay in the car.

He pretended not to see the surprised look on Maisel's face, got out and took the few steps towards the front entrance. The Field Marshal must have seen the car approaching and greeted him at the door. General Burgdorf felt he owed it to the Field Marshal to deliver the Fuehrer's decision in private and to give the Field Marshal time to compose himself before he told his wife and son. Burgdorf looked out of the hall window whilst the Field Marshal went upstairs. He heard the muffled cries of the Field Marshal's wife coming from upstairs, a door closing and footsteps on the staircase. The Field Marshal's son accompanied his father outside. Field Marshal Rommel hugged him one last time, whispered to him and kissed him on the head. Maisel was still in the car but the driver held the door open for Field Marshal Rommel, who took the seat at the back. Burgdorf climbed in and sat beside him.

Now, contrary to his orders, Burgdorf agreed to the Field Marshal's request for a last walk in the woods. It was here that he used to hunt rabbits and deer with his son Manfred on the days he was back from the Front. Hunting had been their excuse to spend time together, just father and son. They would sit at the end of the clearing, marvelling at a deer grazing or the occasional stag sniffing at the morning mist. Not a word would be spoken then, sitting still and hoping the animals would not get their scent.

Now both men entered the forest. The Field Marshal stopped and took several deep breaths, filling his lungs with the smell of the tall pine trees which now shielded them from view.

'It is time Field Marshal.'

'Is this what it has come down to? Ten minutes with my family was all I was allowed?'

'It will be painless and quick.' General Burgdorf put his hand into his jacket pocket and took out a small capsule, opened his hand and showed it to the Field Marshal.

'By painless I assume that you mean no physical pain? Burgdorf do I have your word about my family?'

'You have my word, I will see to it myself, but we must return to the car now, I can see the *Waffen SS* striding towards us.'

Field Marshal Rommel turned towards the car in the distance and started walking down the hill towards it. Burgdorf nodded to Maisel and the driver. Both of them got out of the car and walked away. Field Marshal Rommel took his seat again at the back with Burgdorf next to him and the Field Marshal took the small capsule from Burgdorf's outstretched hand.

The radio announcement started with the sombre military funeral march:

'Citizens of the German Reich. It is my painful duty to inform you that Field Marshal Erwin Rommel has, on this day, the 14th of October 1944, succumbed to his injuries sustained in an attack by the British Air Force in France in July of this year. A State funeral will be held in Ulm on the 18th of October. Our Fuehrer expressed his sorrow and has sent his sympathy to the Field Marshal's family. Our Fuehrer in his statement proclaimed that the Country has lost one of the greatest officers of all time.'

14th October 1944
Late afternoon
Hildesheim, Germany

The announcement was still ringing in my ears. Earlier on we had heard the rumours at the school gate when we collected the children at the end of the day. I refused to believe what the other mothers had heard.

'Maria, this cannot be true, how could it? We have previously heard Rommel was recovering well.'

She looked at me with concern. 'What if it is true Hilde, what if he is dead?'

'The Field Marshal cannot be dead. Has time not shown him to be invincible?'

Back at our apartment Frau Bucker had not heard anything about it. Klaus went upstairs to ask her to come down. She came running, taking two steps at a time.

'What do you mean, Field Marshal Rommel is dead?' she asked out of breath.

Maria, meanwhile, had found the *Broadcast from the Front-Line* station, which was giving daily updates of what was happening in various parts of the world where our troops were fighting their battles. We would normally not tune into this broadcast, most of it was propaganda, but if there was any truth to this rumour, this station would have to report it.

After we had heard the announcement there was total silence in the room. Klaus had re-joined Renate, Karl-Heinz, Hugo and Manfred at the kitchen table, where they sat with their slices of bread and glasses of milk.

Finally Frau Bucker spoke. 'Hilde, what will happen to us all? As long as the Field Marshal was alive, there was hope, don't you think?'

I hardly heard what she said. I was looking towards the kitchen window as my mind drifted back.

Chapter 1

Spring 1926
Tilsit, East Prussia

'Hilde, what is keeping you?' I heard my mother calling me from inside the house.

There was no school today and I was day-dreaming again, feeding the chickens and pigs on our small-holding back home. At last my father had found a job at the new railway company which had set up their headquarters here in our town up in the North East of the country. My mother thought it would never happen: my father working again. She knew the physical pain of losing his right arm, at the end of the 1914-1918 War, would fade and if we all helped he could continue to work the land.

But my father just sat inside, staring at a blank wall or out of the window at the fields, hardly acknowledging our presence.

The winter had been particularly hard. Normally the frost would last from October to March, but this year the river was still frozen in the middle of April.

The *Memel*, which is the large river going right through our home town, can be a busy shipping lane when the ice has gone. Almost everything will then have to be transported via flat loading vessels. Coal, wood, big crates of fish, caught fresh that morning in the Baltic Sea, sacks containing flour, potatoes, vegetables, all going to and from our little harbour.

When the river is frozen solid, it is used as a shortcut to go from one side to the other.

Most houses and small-holdings were east of the river, but the schools, market square, town hall, weekly stalls and small shops were on the west side.

The only two bridges were spaced quite far apart, therefore for people to get across it was a lengthy journey. Normal transport would be by horse and cart, but most commonly you walked and pulled your cart to take your produce to the market and buy the needed supplies.

When the ice was declared safe at Christmas time, the market stores would be on the ice itself. There would be big metal drums with fires to provide light and warm places to huddle around. Stalls would sell hot drinks, cocoa for the children and grog (rum, sugar and hot water) for the adults. Others sold roasted chestnuts, sausages and smoked fish.

Winters were very long and dark. For several weeks a year we only had sunlight for about four hours a day. Any ice skating, which we children loved, could only take place on Sundays after church.

This is why we skated long into spring, even though the ice was starting to melt.

Last Spring, when we all went skating for one last time, before we could not risk it any longer, my cousin Norbert went out too far and the ice gave away under his weight. It was already getting dark and we did not see him going under.

He came back to the surface and managed to shout for help but before we could get there he had gone again. We got as near to the hole as we could. All the time the ice was cracking beneath us. My brother Arno suggested we lay flat on our bellies and to pull ourselves forward the last few meters. This took slightly longer but finally we reached into the icy water.

It seemed a long time, but when he came up again, four pairs of hands grabbed his coat, determined not to let go.

In shock and exhausted he reached up and we managed to pull him out.

It was a long walk home, his coat was very heavy and he took it off, his skates were gone, he was only wearing his socks.

My aunt boiled kettles of water, put him in a bath in front of the fire and sent us home.

6

My mother ran over to her house as soon as we told her. There was nothing to eat for us that night, but we did not even notice.

Norbert had a high temperature the next day and by the evening he was in a coma. The doctor was called but my mother said he shook his head and told them to pray. Norbert died of pneumonia three days later.

The day we buried Norbert was the first day my father left the house after his return from the War.

I collected the fresh eggs, only eight, my mother would be unhappy, two hens had stopped laying. There will be no point in keeping them.

Today we have one of our favourite meals for dinner: meatballs, cabbage and boiled potatoes. We always wait until my father comes back from work and I nervously look out of the kitchen window because I knew my teacher would be coming over in the early evening.

I had been selected by the local theatre to sing the main part in an opera, Hansel and Gretel, and I was Gretel. I did not even have to audition; this was my third main role in fourteen months. But the performing group would be travelling around the country and for that I needed permission from my school and my parents.

Next term I was going to join the Theatre School run by the Performing Arts Centre.

Herr Potenski arrived about 7 pm; unannounced because I lacked the courage to tell my parents. I knew my mother would normally take the side of the children, but this time I was not so sure. And as for my father, although he could be mellow at times, watch out if he had stopped at the local drinking house before he returned home, those were the evenings our meals were either eaten cold, warmed up or not at all. Those evenings seemed to occur more frequently in recent months.

My little sister Erika, my elder brothers Arno, Helmut and Herbert, would all disappear and hide in the back yard, pretending to be busy with the animals.

Tonight, unfortunately, was one of those evenings. The evening would not always turn out the same. After his first drink, his depression would ease. Another one or two and he would really get jolly.

He would tell anecdotes, make up stories, tell jokes; like the entertainer I had seen at a local fair. At the end he would always sing an old melancholic folk song. We children would sit on the floor, loving every bit of it, but silently praying that he would stop the drinks before his mood would change.

My teacher arrived before my father and was now sitting at our kitchen table, where my mother had put an extra plate out to accommodate our guest.

I spotted my father noisily opening the front gate, trying to steady himself.

As if on cue, Helmut took Erika's hand and my three brothers and sister slipped out through the back. I shrugged my shoulders, looking back at them and decided to stay with my mother and my teacher.

'What on earth is going on?' my father shouted when he came into the kitchen.

'It's alright August. Herr Potenski is here to talk about the permission needed for Hilde to travel with the theatre group.'

'Too late for that. Goodbye Herr Potenski,' slurred my father, stumbling, hoping to recover his balance by trying to reach out for the table, temporarily forgetting there was no right arm to reach out with. Confusion and terror showing on his face, pleading eyes staring at my mother as he fell.

'What do you mean it's too late?' my teacher demanded to know.

'Hilde has work to go to in Berlin and she is leaving next week.' My mother never looked at me when she said it.

Chapter 2

Erika held me tight and clung on to me during my last night at home, not wanting to let me go.

'Are you really going to leave us?' She was crying now. I moved her closer towards me in our shared bed. Next to our bed on my left-hand side, in her cot, our baby sister Gisela, who had been fretting for the last hour, keeping us awake. Not that we could have slept anyway.

'I will be coming home all the time to see you. Think about the beautiful things I can bring back from Berlin.' I sounded more confident than I was, not wanting to show my own fear and apprehension.

Who would now look after the girls? I was their big sister and I felt responsible for the younger girls. Yes my brothers would do their best but sometimes little girls just needed their sister.

My mother was not a woman of many words . As she helped me pack earlier in the afternoon, she gave me little advice on what I was going to face away from the relative safety of my home. I loved my home, loved looking after the animals and loved school. Foolishly I thought it would last forever.

All I knew by now was that my elder sister Helene had found me a position in a household in Berlin.

I was up before everybody else and went outside to feed the animals one last time. Two hens were missing, our supper last night. I could not bring myself to eat any of it.

My father got really angry, struck the table with his fist, making all the plates and dishes jump up. The water jug tipped over soaking the potatoes. He stood up, pointing at me with his fork, shouting at me that I was ungrateful and that I should be thankful all the family had come over for a dinner especially cooked for me.

My aunt stood up, but my uncle put his hand on her shoulder and told her to sit down.

Erika left her seat, ran over to me and sat on my lap. My mother never said a word.

'Erika! Get back to your chair and finish your dinner!' my father said through gritted teeth. He was furious now. You could see the veins on his red, angry face.

I stood up, lifted Erika into my arms, faced my father and for the first time was not afraid of him. 'I don't live here anymore.' I walked out of the kitchen but did not dare to look back.

My father had left for work before I got back into the kitchen, not bothering to say goodbye. The clothes I was taking with me were in a cardboard box on the kitchen floor. The box looked sturdy and to make it easier for me to carry had a string around it and a makeshift handle. I lifted it up again wondering how I would get it to Berlin in one piece.

It was going to be a difficult long journey. I had never travelled further than *Koenigsberg*, which was very close to the German/Polish border. I had looked at the map at school when I said my farewells to teachers and friends. Herr Potenski had been very kind and covered my route with the rest of the class, making me promise to keep in touch. It would be about 860 km from my hometown to Berlin. First I had to take the small local train from *Tilsit* to *Koenigsberg*. There I had to change to the Prussia Eastern Railway Line, which started off in Warsaw. The line was just one track which meant one train going out every two days.

The train was always very full, especially at this time of the year. May was the month the first harvests were sent to the bigger towns, farmers would travel for days to sell their goods. This area was famous for white asparagus and cheese.

We had to walk from the house to the station. Three-year-old Erika was adamant she was not going to be left behind. 'I will come with you to Berlin' she insisted.

'You can't come to work with me but would you like to see the train?' I knelt down to be her height, and looked into her eyes, when I replied.

Arno lifted her onto our cart and she was allowed to sit on my box. My mother ran inside and got a blanket to put around her. The wind from the east struck our faces and stung our eyes. My brothers only had their jumpers to protect them and nothing on their hands and heads. My mother had given me her coat, brown fur, which she had for as long as I could remember. I had a headscarf wrapped tightly around me, gloves, and I was given a pair of boots.

I hugged my mother and told her I would send a message as soon as I could, kissed baby Gisela and was ready to leave.

The roads from our house to the town were small dirt tracks and it was difficult to move the cart. Arno and Helmut were pulling in the front and Herbert pushing from the back.

I saw my aunt and cousins running towards us, my aunt shouting all the way.

'Wait! Wait! Elisabeth you go with Hilde, I will watch Gisela.' She bent down, her hands resting on her knees, trying to catch her breath.

We were a strange procession arriving at the station, two hours after leaving home.

My brothers and cousins taking it in turns to push or pull, sweat was now running down their faces. Erika, holding my left hand through the wooden slats of the cart, my mother on my right hand side, neither of them letting go of me.

Chapter 3

There was nowhere for me to sit on the train when I finally managed to heave my box on board, prising away Erika's arms which were firmly locked behind my neck. Inside the train it was hot, dark and very noisy. By now I was glad I insisted my mother took back her fur coat, suggesting she exchanged it with her woollen jacket. She believed me when I told her that, after all, Berlin was so much further south and it would only be in my way because I would have very little opportunity to wear it. I knew she had no other coat and the winters up in the North East are bitterly cold with temperatures of minus 25 degrees Celsius, not counting the icy blast coming from Siberia.

The train arrived in *Koenigsberg* with plenty of time for me to find out where I had to go and get the next one coming from Warsaw going to Berlin. I was right at the door which meant I was one of the first ones trying to get off. I was holding my box with one hand and the door handle with the other but I did not have the strength to open it. People behind me were getting angry and trying to get past me. One more push and the door flew open making me stumble and miss the step down. I fell onto the platform still holding my box. People climbed over me, rushing on. I stayed where I was hoping I would wake up any minute and find that this was just a bad dream.

'*Jak masz na imie?*' a women pulled me to my feet. '*Jak masz na imie?*' she asked me again but this time louder.

'Hilde, my name is Hilde,' I whispered looking up at her. She had a broad smile showing a toothless mouth. Her head was covered with what looked like a selection of scarves. She was wearing several jumpers and a cardigan on top, long patterned skirt, thick socks and open-toed shoes.

Next to her was a lanky boy, whose freckled face was almost covered by an enormous fur hat pulled right over his ears and a thick black jacket with the collar turned up to give extra protection from the wind, Cossack-style trousers and dark boots which reached up to his knees. He looked about my age.

'*Oleg. mi Polski.*' He held out his hand. I took it and felt a firm grip when he shook it.

'*Matka,*' he pointed to his mother who nodded in agreement.

'Where are you going to?' I asked but he looked at me blankly. '*Ktore miasto?*' I repeated best I could, silently thanking Herr Potenski who had the foresight to teach us some of his language.

'*Berlin.*' He searched my face and got a thankful smile in return and a nod from me.

'*You come.*' He looked at his mother as he said it.

I was not quite sure what was happening but he took my box and loaded it onto a wagon which was stacked high with baskets of live chickens. There must have been over twenty baskets each holding at least eight chickens.

We could hear the train arriving before we saw it. A roar and rumble in the distance, followed by a cloud of mist and steam. I held on to Oleg. I feared I would lose him in the damp fog which was all around us, clearing very slowly.

I stepped forward when the train stopped, trying to find the nearest door to get in. '*Nie*' Oleg shook his head and started to push his wagon to the back of the train.

The carriages at the end were from a goods train and we went to the very last one. The sliding door was open and a noisy group of people huddled closely together staring at us.

There was no way we could fit all of us, including the chickens, in there with the others. Several of the men, who were dressed similar to Oleg jumped down and started unloading the wagon, quickly passing basket after basket to outstretched hands.

Strong arms lifted me up and the women pulled me inside. My box was now next to me .A little boy looked at it curiously and after a while claimed it as his stool. The wagon was lifted to the top of the train, joining others upside down, all secured by ropes.

The stench and noise in the cramped carriage made me take a step back but several hands got hold of me before I could fall, fingering my clothes, all speaking at once.

'*Niemka.*' About thirty worried faces stared at me in silence. They had just learned I was German.

Oleg pulled me into the crowd, '*Bliski przyjaciel*' he shouted looking around. I understood the word for 'friend'.

One by one they came forward and took my hand.

The train started to move which made the men stand up, slide the door across, but leaving a space open for light and air. I looked around and found a small space between the baskets of chicken and wooden crates of fresh vegetables. We would not reach Berlin until the following day. I kept myself to myself and tried to sleep.

Despite the acidy overwhelming stench, the noise from the people and animals, I must have dropped off.

I woke when the train made a sudden jerk backwards, the wheels under me screeched and slowly the train came to a complete stop. It was almost dark. Very little light came through the opening of the door, or the small open windows on the other side, secured via metal bars.

I heard voices outside and several carriage doors being opened, ours was the last one. Fresh air streamed in and the men outside shone torches around resting on the faces of my travelling companions.

'Polski!' one of them shouted, laughed and started to climb in. He had not noticed me in the corner. I stood up, my legs shaking, trying to conceal my fear.

'These people are needed in Berlin, they are farmers and the markets have been notified, they will be met when we get there.' I hoped that this sounded feasible and had a ring of truth to it.

'Papers!' he barked, shaking his head. Dozens of trembling hands searched their pockets and produced some sort of cards. He checked only a few, turned to me and said, 'I would be more careful of who your friends are.' He climbed back down and the door was slammed shut.

Finally Oleg recovered. '*Hilde, how old?*' he asked me.

'*Czternascie.*' I am fourteen, I replied.

Oleg's mother made her way over to me, held my hands and pointed to some bread which was partly covered by a piece of cloth. Yes, I was hungry, I nodded, but first I needed a toilet.

'*Toateta*?' Several fingers pointed to a bucket in the other corner which I had not noticed before. It was slightly hidden by the straw on the floor and explained some of the smell I had not yet got used to. I must have looked horrified as one by one they turned their faces in the opposite direction and then the first child started laughing. Soon there were roars of laughter. I think mine was the loudest.

Chapter 4

22nd May 1928
My 16th Birthday
Berlin

Helene came over to see me last week. She had come back from a visit to see our family and brought me a parcel from our mother. I had not been home since I arrived in Berlin. I did not even know I had a new baby sister called Grete.

I was given the Saturday after my birthday off. Frau von Buelow had called me upstairs and given me a gift: a white damask serviette with my initial embroidered on. Folded inside were two movie tickets, for a film called *Hara-kiri*. I had heard about it but never imagined I would be able to see it.

I loved going upstairs, I would sneak there when the house was empty, pretending it was mine. I marvelled at the photographs. On the large wall were photos of Marie von Buelow in her movie rolls and theatre plays. Most intriguing were the ones on the grand piano in silver frames. There were several of Tchaikovsky alone and also some of him together with Marie and her late husband Hans. One of them was taken after a concert in Saint Petersburg, which Hans von Buelow had directed and played in, as the soloist in the Piano Concerto No 1.

Frau von Buelow once spotted me when I was looking at the photos. I was startled because I did not hear her entering the room. I feared instant dismissal but instead she kindly explained every photo to me and asked me whether I liked the art. This was my opportunity to tell her about my singing.

Besides a footman and the gardener, I was the only one in the household and soon learned to judge her mood when she returned

16

from her outings. If she seemed sad to me I would cook meals using Polish recipes which reminded her of her childhood.

I waited for my actual birthday to open my parcel from my mother. Inside was a metal box. It was mainly black but had a red and gold stripe around the lid. The lid had a handle in the middle which folded down. It had a lock and a key. Inside the box was a letter from my mother, letters from my brothers and a drawing from Erika. There were birthday cards from my school friends and a long letter from Herr Potenski with encouraging words. I cried when I ate my favourite biscuits which my mother had included.

I had sent a message to Oleg via *Rohr post* (pneumatic tube). These were widely used throughout Berlin and were a quick way of getting letters delivered.

Oleg now spent a lot of time in Berlin with his aunt and uncle, who had a Polish food shop. His family still came by train from Poland every two weeks to sell their farm products. He was getting very concerned about his mother. The journeys were long and it was beginning to get very dangerous.

Oleg told me that last time they travelled by train with the chickens to go to their usual market, a group of youths stormed the train when it arrived in Berlin, running amok through the carriages, tipping over every box and basket they could reach. They then homed in on Oleg's mother, who was already on the platform, pushed her over in front of an oncoming train. Only the quick reactions by the other farmers diverted a disaster.

The youth shouted and laughed. 'Go home, Polskis then opened some of the baskets and let the chickens escape. Oleg did not let his mother come back for almost 6 months. I felt very ashamed when he told me and found it hard to look into his eyes, yet alone speak to his mother.

The movie theatre was located at the Alexander Platz. I could get there by train, The *S-Bahn*. I had met Oleg there one time before. I did not know whether he would be there or whether he received my note which I had sent two days ago.

Although I spotted him in the distance, I could hardly believe my eyes. He stood there wearing a suit, with a waistcoat and a tie and in his hands he had a bunch of white lilacs. He shuffled his feet nervously when I approved, shrugged his shoulders and said, 'My uncle's clothes.'

We had become the very best of friends. Both of us were far away from home, taking comfort from each other. If my sister Helene knew that my best friend was Polish, she did not let on, I trusted her enough to know she would not tell our father.

Chapter 5

Cold, so cold, cold and dark, my teeth chattered, my clothes were soaking and still I continued. Thoughts were racing through my head, why did I believe in him? A wave hit my body and the water rose up to my chest. It took my breath away and my heart missed a beat or two. Not much further now and I would be completely swallowed up by the freezing water. I heard the church clock, 1 o'clock in the morning. I could not swim.

I met Alfred on a sunny morning. I was waiting for Oleg at our usual place. We had arranged to meet at the little café opposite the picture house. We had made friends with the owner Harel and his wife Karina, whose families lived in Poland not far from my home town. It felt strangely comfortable to have a circle of friends from the same region. You never had to feel alone or deserted. We used to swap old stories and heard the latest news. I could see my home in my mind when we talked and if I closed my eyes just for a second, I could see my mother and smell the cooking in our kitchen.

Oleg did not show up and by now I was pacing up and down trying to figure out why he wasn't here. Always imagining the worst, I worried about him all the time, I knew his German was getting better, but when he spoke you could still hear his strong accent.

'Go and sit down, Hilde, he will be here in a minute.' Even when he said it, Harel himself did not look that convinced and kept looking back and forth towards the door.

The café was really getting busy, people coming and going. I did not like to sit on my own and hesitated slightly before I found a small table where I could watch the Square.

I did not have a lot of time, I had made some excuses this morning, said I knew the fish stall would have a fresh delivery today. Now I hoped it was true, I had put fish on the menu for tonight and Frau von Buelow had guests.

'Are you waiting for someone?' A stranger looked at me. I turned round to see whether I could spot Harel, but he was nowhere in sight.

I just stared at him, not knowing what to answer, his face looked kind and he had a disarming smile, stretched out his hand whilst he said, ' My name is Alfred, do you mind if I sit down?' For a while he stood there and finally decided he would just join me. 'Sorry but all other seats are taken.'

Harel came over, looked at me, put a cup of coffee in front of me 'Hilde, are you alright?' he asked whilst he took Alfred's order.

'Fraeulein Hilde, I'll just have my breakfast and I am off, I won't bother you. Promise.' He added with a cheeky grin. I started to relax a little. You had to be really careful, when you spoke to strangers these days, especially when your friends were from Poland.

I could not wait much longer, if I wanted to go to the fish stall and be back in time to finish the housework and start the cooking. I stood up and went over to Harel, who assured me he would try to find out why Oleg had not come and he would be in touch.

I heard a car horn right beside me just as I was going to cross the street. The sound made me take a step backwards and I almost collided with an old lady. I lost the grip of my basket and the potatoes and onions rolled into the street. The driver jumped out, apologising profusely, bent down and started to pick up my shopping. He looked up and I realised it was Alfred.

'Are you following me?' I was beginning to get cross instead of worried.

'At least let me drive you home Fraeulein Hilde.' Alfred again displayed his charming smile. He was driving a Ford, said it was a model 'T'. On the way back to the house he told me there was a new factory in Berlin where these cars were assembled from parts brought over from America and he was one of the test drivers.

20

I asked him to let me out at the bottom of the road, I did not want anybody to see me arriving in a car, nor did I want Alfred to know where I lived.

He did not let me go without a promise we would have a coffee the following week. I suggested *Sanssousi* which was an old summer palace of *Frederick the Great* with large gardens and nice cafés. This was to the west of my workplace and I could go there by bicycle.

Alfred insisted he was going to pick me up exactly where he dropped me off.

I found it easy to talk to him but avoided talking about my friends. He told me about his work at the factory, about his childhood, his hometown of Hamburg, his brothers and sisters. There were musicians playing at the café and we danced, I even tried my first glass of wine.

On the way home he held my hand some of the time, steering just with his left hand. At the bottom of the road, he put his hand under my chin, raised my head and kissed me softly on the lips. I had never been kissed before.

I could not wait to see him again, and all thoughts of Oleg went out of the window. I was totally and utterly in love, a feeling I had not experienced before. I tried to meet him as often as I could and was overwhelmed by his generosity. He showered me with little gifts. Once he surprised me with a silver necklace, with the letter 'H' as a pendant. Another time he brought me a brooch which was like a lizard; and lots of chocolates and flowers. Not once did he come to see me empty handed. I imagined myself being married and having a family of my own, visualised myself in a rocking chair in front of a fire cradling a infant, in one of those large houses down the street.

The chocolates were starting to take a toll on my body, so I asked him not to bring them so often although I loved the taste. I always kept them in my mouth for as long as I could, letting them melt slowly. He gave me a curious look and went quiet.

A message arrived from Harel. I was to come and see him at the café. Again I combined it with a visit to the fish stall. I went there first to make sure they sold smoked eel that day. I felt slightly nauseated and dizzy from the smell of fish. I had to hold onto a lamppost to regain my balance. Just before I got to the café, I saw a couple entering, a man in uniform with a heavily pregnant women holding on to his arm. They took the seat at the window.

I froze when I reached for the door handle, the man looked at me, it was my Alfred. I had not seen him for two weeks. He told me he had to travel to deliver a car. He was wearing a brown shirt with an emblem armband - a uniform. The woman next to him saw him looking at me and turned her head. I stumbled and had tears streaming down my face, my heart pounding so hard it hurt. People were parting to let me through, I no longer cared.

I did not drown myself, that cold November morning. Trance-like I waded back to the bank of the river and walked through the deserted streets. Back at the house, I took off my wet clothes and put them in the bath tub behind the kitchen, then I took an empty brown beer bottle with a stopper which was held by a metal clip. If you did not make the water too hot, you could fill it without cracking the glass and it made a good hot water bottle. In bed I held the bottle and pressed it against my stomach.

A sharp pain woke me after a few hours and I managed to get back downstairs to the kitchen, boiled some water, took the wet clothes out of the tub and filled it with as much hot water as possible. All the while blood was running down my legs, and for a moment I did not worry how much noise I made. I lowered myself into the hot bath, my skin slightly tingling but my cramps seemed to ease a little. I bit into the towel so that I would not scream and felt lumps leaving my body. I had no strength to look.

It was by now getting light, I would have to get out to start making the fires and preparing the breakfast. I just left everything as it was, got out of the bath and went back upstairs. I got dressed and started my day's work.

Chapter 6

Christmas 1930

'Coming-Home-Christmas-Hilde' read the telegram I sent my mother. I promised Marie von Buelow I would be back straight after New Year's Eve, just in time to help with the preparation for the commemorations concerts being arranged to honour her late husband's 100th anniversary. This would be the first time in four years that I was going home. I was loaned warm clothing: a grey *Loden mantel*, which originally came from Bavaria and had little green felt patches with white edelweiss emblems on the pockets. The coat reached almost to the floor, which I loved. Harel gave me a brown fur lined hat and a black scarf and gloves.

'Well thank you Alfred' I thought when I managed to change his silver necklace for a pair of second hand boots on the black market. The boots laced up above my ankle, they were a little too large, but with thick socks I would manage just fine. Alfred's lizard brooch was swapped for a rucksack. Now I was glad I did not throw these gifts into the river *Spree* that dreadful night last month.

I got Oleg's home address from Harel. Word had it that he was not coming back to Berlin. I had no papers which would allow me to travel to Poland, but I wanted the address just in case. I memorised all the details from the written slip, which was difficult because some of the writing I did not understand, but I hoped I could ask Herr Potenski and prayed he was still living at his old place.

I reached Tilsit late afternoon on the second day. It had snowed most of the way and the train had to stop several times, people jumped off and cleared away the snow drifts - some people using bare hands, others emptied crates and used them as make-do shovels. The snow was almost up to my knees when I got on to the platform, I wondered how I would find the strength to wade through it the long way to our house. Moonshine lit my way, the white country before me was glittering like a thousand stars had fallen from the sky. The North Star was right above. I pretended it was a protecting eye watching every step of mine.

Erika opened the door after several knocks. 'Mamma, there is a soldier.' She did not recognise me in my heavy clothes, the coat almost invisible, covered in snow. Some sticking to my hat which was pulled down making the features of my face disappear.

'Erika, it's me' I sobbed but the tears froze on my face before they could reach my chin.

'Mamma' she ran inside instead of towards me. Herbert rushed forward; or at least I thought that must be Herbert, instead of a skinny boy, a young man pulled me in and hugged me tight.

My mother nearly dropped the goose she was stuffing with apples, preparing tomorrow's Christmas lunch. I was now leaving wet puddles of melting snow on the kitchen floor. Helmut shook his head in disbelief and took my wet coat, I gave him the gloves and scarf and he placed everything over the wooden rack in front of the open fire, after he removed half dried nappies and baby clothes.

'What are you doing here?' My mother had finally found her voice.

'I sent you a telegram,' I replied, trying to see Erika who was hiding behind my mother. Only now I noticed my mother's stooped back, her lifeless eyes, hands red raw from the cold and hard work, her small body almost disappearing underneath the frayed large cardigan which definitely belonged to my father, who was nowhere to be seen.

'Erika, will you show me your little sister?' I moved towards her and kissed my mother on the cheek.

'Which one?' Erika realised I had not registered what she said and repeated 'Which one? 'The little one or the baby?' My heart sank, another baby, no wonder my mother looked so worn out.

'Both of course,' I gave her a reassuring smile.

'Do you want to see my baby brother as well?' she skipped off not waiting for a reply.

The three month old twins, Guenter and Traute, were in separate drawers, taken out from the chest and placed side by side on the ground. Two year old Grete was in the cot. Where was Gisela who was now nearly five? Erika pointed towards the bed. I looked underneath and large frightened eyes stared back and the small body moved further towards the wall, like a young doe caught in the lights of a train.

'She thinks you are Father Christmas, Mamma told her he knew if you had been naughty.' She rolled her eyes, being seven you are far too grown up to believe in Father Christmas, her look said so.

Erika and Gisela loved the ribbons I bought them and sweaters I had knitted. Erika did not take hers off and slept in it. I hoped her favourite colour was still lilac. I had found two fabric fairies in the department store and carefully stitched them on, but leaving the wings untouched. Erika pretended to fly.

The hot soup on Christmas Eve finally brought life back into my numb body. I fell asleep in my old bed covered by two little sisters, who laid their bodies across mine, like a welcoming blanket.

All night my mother was up with the twins. When I got into the kitchen in the morning Arno had one of the babies on his lap with a feeding bottle. My mother had the other.

'Now you are back home, you can stay and help your mother,' was all I got from my father.

I turned to Arno, 'Does Herr Potenski still teach at the school?'

'That is Hilde alright, always caring about everybody besides her own flesh and blood. Well, no, that Polski went back where he came from. Joined the Polish Army, can't believe we ever let them live here in the first place,' my father ranted on.

I knew what I wanted to reply, but I bit my lips after I saw the fear in my mother's eyes.

My mother had done miracles with the little food there was. Erika, Gisela and I took care of the smaller children to give my mother a well-earned rest. My brothers made sure the animals had been taken care of and that there was enough dry wood in the house for the fire as lots of hot water was needed for the constant arrival of dirty nappies. The water was boiled in a large kettle which sat on top of the cooker. My father had gone out after dinner, I assume to the local drinking house, but not before he made Herbert and Helmut take the shovels out front to clear a walkway through the newly settled snow.

Erika did not say goodbye to me: she had been in hiding all morning, I was leaving her behind again and she felt betrayed. This time it was my mother who wanted me to stay and it was me who wanted to leave.

Chapter 7

I could not cast my vote on Federal Election Day, March of 1933. My twenty-first birthday was some months away plus I was still officially registered in my home town. The last two years had taken their toll with many people out of work and men in the streets growing very restless.

I did not like to go out after dark and hurried back as soon as I finished my task in town. Not a day went by when I did not pass hungry mothers with children queuing for the little hand-outs there were.

I was to help out at a party that evening on the other side of town. The car collected me late afternoon. The cook in charge of the dinner had asked for me by name and as long as I had my work done at Frau van Buelow's, I was allowed to go.

I went straight into the kitchen to find out why I was here and what I was supposed to do.

I recognised Oleg's cousin Anna straight away, having met her previously at Harel's café. She gave me a knowing look, but both of us did not openly acknowledge each other. We dared not exchange any words other than conversations regarding the preparation of the evening meal. Silently we chopped vegetables, peeled potatoes and put the roasting chickens in the oven.

I helped to serve the starters of white asparagus, with a boiled egg covered in a mustard-flavoured sauce. I almost dropped one of the plates when I realised whose house I was in and whose dinner party this was. It had never occurred to me to check or ask Anna when I arrived. I immediately recognised this was *Lil Dagover* the German film actress. I would never forget the first time I went to see a movie all that time ago. Today's celebration was the success of her first English film *The Woman from Monte Carlo*. There was going to be a showing of it later and I hoped we would be able to sneak in without being noticed.

'How is he?' I finally ask Anna, between serving the last course of chocolate pudding with vanilla cream and keeping an eye on the boiling kettle for the coffee.

Anna reached into her skirt pocket, which was covered by her white apron and gave me a letter. At last, a note from Oleg. I quickly took it and would read it later when I got back to my room.

In the dining room I overheard some conversations about the election which was taking place. I tried to make out what was said but as soon as I was spotted, the room went quiet.

'Anna, do you know what is happening out there?' I pointed towards the street but she just gave me a puzzled look. 'The election, I mean.'

'No good will come from it Hilde, I am thinking of returning to Warsaw. If you have a message, pass it on to Harel as soon as you can, I will try and pick it up before I leave.' Anna busied herself with cleaning one of the large roasting tins.

'Do they know you are leaving?' Her look told me otherwise.

The same car which picked me up took me back at midnight. It was total chaos outside. People were running through the streets trying to block our way, shaking their fists, some people had lit fires. We came across a group of men waving flags.

'Please ask them what is happening,' I leaned forward towards the driver.

'We should just keep going and get you home Fraulein,' was his reply. But he stopped and slightly opened the car door. He spoke to a young man in uniform, closed the door and kept on driving. 'The National Socialist German Workers Party got a lot more votes than expected, but did not get a majority.' I could pick up his Polish accent in his shaking voice.

We crossed the Alexander Platz, which was besieged by people. Out of the corner of my eyes I could spot Harel's café, surrounded by a group of men clearly laughing.

'Stop! Stop the car!' I opened the door and jumped onto the pavement before the driver stopped completely. I fell onto the ground but quickly recovered and ran towards Harel's place. All the windows had painted marks on them. 'What is this?' I asked the person next to me.

'A swastika Fraulein, the symbol of the National Socialist Party,' was his reply.

I moved forward and touched the paint, it was still wet and I stared at my red fingers which looked like I had cut myself and could not stop bleeding. I took off my cardigan and started to wipe the paint off the door. Nobody spoke but angry looks were shot in my direction like daggers cutting into me.

'Fraulein, we had better be going,' the worried-looking driver tapped me on my shoulders, but I brushed him off and carried on more furiously now. I recognised some of Oleg's customers. Tears started to form in my eyes, but I fought them as best I could.

'Please get the apron from my bag, so that these good people can help me,' I replied instead.

One by one they turned away and left. The driver and I started to clean the windows together, just leaving red unrecognisable smudges.

Chapter 8

Harel crouched underneath the upstairs window and watched the events unfolding in the Square. He woke up around midnight, thought he heard a noise downstairs, it sounded like banging against the door. He looked over to where Karina was sleeping. She had been worried most of the day and all evening, their little boy would not settle tonight and she was concerned about his high temperature. They had tried to get the doctor but he did not come, although Oleg himself went there three times.

The crowd of people grew larger, he tried to listen to what they were shouting, but he could not quite figure it out.

He saw the large car arriving and stopping, then Hilde rushing out, falling, getting up and carrying on towards his café. He could not see straight down unless he opened the window.

He knew Hilde would be in the area tonight, Anna had told him, still he was wondering what she was doing here this time of night. He was tempted to creep downstairs to have a better look and he knew it was cowardice not to do it. He looked over to Karina again, still sleeping soundly, and wondered whether he should insist that she leave Berlin and go to live with her mother in Warsaw. They had talked about it in the last few weeks, they knew the Federal Elections were due this month and there was a lot of propaganda in favour of the National Socialist Workers Party.

Now the driver was getting out of the car, walking towards the cafe and disappeared from Harel's view. Then it grew strangely quiet. He hoped Hilde was alright. He would have to go down and check. Maybe it was her banging on the door trying to get in. He realised people started to leave, looking back at the café as they did so.

He felt movement behind him. Karina had woken up and leaned against his body. He kissed her on the top of her head and pulled her towards him.

'What are you doing here, at the window, Harel? Is that Hilde? Harel, is she covered in blood?' Karina shouted the last sentence, waking up their son who started to cry.

Harel pushed her aside, turned around towards the door and took two steps down at a time. He could not see through the café doors or the windows, they were covered in red smudges. His heart sank, he should have come down straight away .He could not believe those German workers would attack a young German woman. His hands were shaking badly, it took him a while to unlock the door. He ran outside shouting Hilde's name, just as she entered the car and it drove off.

Chapter 9

I unfolded Oleg's letter as soon as I was in my room. The footman had been waiting for me to come back in. He never did this before and did not explain why he was still up. His face, which was normally red from the sun this time of the year, paled visibly when he saw me. I went straight into the bathroom, behind the kitchen and left my cardigan and apron on the floor, just where they fell. All energy was drained from me.

When I got back into the kitchen a hot cup of tea was waiting for me. My hands were shaking when I put it towards my mouth immediately smelling the delicious strength of black rum. The sweetness of the strong tea calmed my nerves.

'The driver told me what you did Hilde, you are very brave but also very foolish.' The footman told me when he joined me at the table. 'Frau von Buelow must not know about it, she might get compromised,' he continued. I have an aunt living in the Harz Mountains, she is looking for a help, I think you should go.' He looked at me.

'Can you tell me what is happening?' I asked him in reply.

I could see in his face, his thoughts seemed to be racing in his head, not sure whether he could trust me. After a pause he decided to reply.

'The National Workers Party is getting stronger and stronger. They did not win tonight but it will only be a matter of time. You have seen with your own eyes what is happening in the streets. If Hitler gets into power, God help us, Hilde.' His face was grim and he looked a little bit nervous when he spoke.

'What about my friends and what about my work? I can't just leave!' I had never had a conversation with him this openly.

'You go when I find your replacement. I will find a reason why you had to leave. You cannot protect your friends Hilde, they must decide for themselves. But by all means warn them.' He got up ready to leave.

'Herr Ludwig,' I had never said his first name before, 'where are the Harz Mountains?'

I savoured every word in Oleg's letter and felt sad when he told me that his mother had not been well for a long time. He and his two brothers were looking after the crops in the fields and the animals because his mother was now no longer able to do the weekly weeding. The green bean season had been especially hard. Picking these was back-breaking work at the best of times, but now they had to check every little bush again and again being careful not to miss any. He was staying at home, whilst his brothers did the market runs. I read between the lines, that his brothers would be here at the market this week. I would go there. Oleg had met a young woman called Ludmilla, whose father had the local store, selling food and household wares. Oleg had met them when he did a delivery. Ludmilla's father had asked him to come inside as he wanted to discuss some business with him. He was opening another shop in Sierakow which was about 10 km away and wanted Oleg to deliver there and to some other stalls he was in contact with. Ludmilla's father had a small lorry and said if Oleg agreed he could use it. He had spent the last few weeks learning how to drive it.

Chapter 10

I gave Oleg's brothers my new address and told them what was happening. Through Oleg's new venture of delivering their goods to stores and other market traders in their local area, from now on, there would be no need for them to travel all this way to Berlin.

Harel was more difficult to persuade to go back home. He had built himself a successful café here in Berlin, which now had loyal customers and although the recent events had shaken him badly, he wanted to stay. Karina - who never saw any bad in anybody – stubbornly refused to listen. She wanted her son to become German, even joked about it, pointing out his blue eyes and blond curls. A throw-back from her great-grandparents, apparently.

'Look, he understands German!' she proudly demonstrated a few heavily accented words, and the little boy smiled obediently.

I got a Rohr post from my sister Helene, saying we should meet up and suggested the new Café Kranzler which had just opened on Kuerfuerstendamm. I had not seen my sister for a long time and this would be my chance to tell her about my plans.

There was no time to reply to her letter and I simply turned up hoping she would be there when she said.

I would not have recognised her, if she had not spotted me. She saw me coming through the door and waved at me fanatically. She sat next to a young man.

She looked wonderful, her hair was cut to a fashionable bob slightly wavy, like the ones I had seen on the latest movie posters. She was wearing dark red lipstick and earrings. Her hat was oblong and flat with a contrast velvet trim, worn slightly on the right side and down a little bit covering her eyes and was almost matching her dark woollen coat with an enormous fur collar. It was quite warm in the café, Still she did not take it off.

'Fraulein,' the young man stood up, bowed, took my hand and kissed it. He then pulled my chair back and I sat down, hoping he did not spot my unpolished shoes. I gave Helene a questioned look and she could not contain her smile any longer.

'Hilde, meet my fiancé Frank,' my sister finally spoke. 'Frank is a schoolteacher and we are getting married in the autumn.'

'Nice to meet you, Frank. Does our father know?' I asked, raising my eyebrows.

We were interrupted by a waiter, who pushed a small trolley with delicious but expensive looking cakes. I looked at the table in front of me, and spotted two half eaten cakes and cups of coffee.

'I'll have a piece of cheesecake and a coffee please,' I said with confidence, hoping a teacher's salary would take care of it.

'How did the two of you meet?' I took a closer look at Frank. He looked as though he had not had a decent meal for a while, well, my sister would take care of that soon. My mother had taught us how to cook. He kept pushing his tortoiseshell rimmed glasses back up his nose, a nervous gesture, I reckoned. He was wearing a dark suit and tie. His hat was on the empty chair next to him.

'At a dance,' she looked very pleased with herself.

'You, dance?' I started to see Helene in a completely different light. I got my answer by watching her face and ignored the daggers which were shot in my direction.

'Frank, what do you teach and where do you live?' I bypassed my sister and went directly to her fiancé.

'Hilde, slow down. Frank is already worried about me taking him home to meet our mother and father. He teaches geography and lives in the Friedrich Strasse. We will both live in his flat when we are married,' my sister stepped in.

She was right of course, why was I worried, both looked so happy. 'Well congratulations. I am really pleased for you.' I raised my coffee cup.

For the rest of the afternoon, I listened to them both talking about their future together and looked at their beaming faces. Helene had sent a letter to our parents, telling them she would be home in two weeks and she was going to bring her fiancé Frank. She hoped I would be able to come to the wedding and Frank made me promise I would. This was not the time to tell her I was moving.

To Helene's surprise I held her for a long time when we parted and asked her to kiss our sisters for me.

Chapter 11

1934

Goslar, Harz Mountains

'*Falling in love again....*' sang Marlene Dietrich, as we listened to
the new V*olksempfaenger* radio – positioned on the small chest of
drawers. Pictures of Frau Lehmann and her late husband on the wall
above.

At almost regular intervals, the music program would be
interrupted and the propaganda Minister Goebbels' voice would
bellow from the speaker, Frau Lehmann would visibly shrink further
into her chair. I could not reach over quickly enough to switch it off.

'Leave it on, Hilde,' she would say, 'we need to hear what he
says, at least then we know to believe the opposite.' She had a
wicked little smile and I hoped her being very outspoken would not
get her into serious trouble.

Sundays were our "special days", as we called them. We had our
little routine by now. First we would listen to the Berlin
Philharmonic which was broadcast around midday. I tried not to
notice the tears forming in her eyes as we did so. She reached for her
handkerchief every time and said, 'I think I am getting a cold, we
had better wrap up warm when we go out.'

The cook would prepare our lunch, and it would always be some
comforting dish from our days living in the North East of the
country. I could not thank Herr Ludwig enough for him sending me
to his aunt, who needed a companion and not 'a help' as he had put
it. After lunch I would get the wheelchair to the front door and help
Frau Lehmann to get comfortable and put a blanket over her knees. I
would push her, or we would walk as she preferred to call it, through

the town past the Square and we would stop at the café not far from the *Kaiserpfalz*, the Old Imperial Palace.

'Madam,' she was always greeted by the owner and our table near the musicians would be ready for us.

Charlotte Lorenzova had played the Cello at the Berlin Philharmonic. That was where she had met her husband Ruediger Lehmann, who played the violin. 'We used to make beautiful music together.' She winked at me when she said it.

When Ruediger was given the chance to form a String Quintet here in Goslar in the Harz Mountains, he jumped at it. Charlotte had just started her music career and enjoyed playing in a large orchestra, a prestigious one like this one in Berlin, of all places to be accepted in.

Ruediger went to Goslar to find somewhere to live. It had to be large enough to include a music room with good acoustics and with enough insulation to not annoy the neighbours. He also needed to find one more violinist and two viola players.

Charlotte decided to follow her heart and they were married at a small synagogue in *Bad Harzburg*, attended by close family and their musician friends. The party was at the Hotel Restaurant '*Parkhof*' which had an association with the synagogue.

'Can I help you?' A handsome young man held the door open for us when we entered the café .It seemed busier than on normal Sundays, some of the small tables had been pushed together forming a long table to one side and a group of about twenty men in uniform occupied most of the chairs.

Frau Lehmann turned her head and shook it, indicating that we should not stay. I was ready to go backwards out of the door when the same young man stopped me.

'Please don't leave. We came to listen to the music. We have a gramophone at our army base and listen to recordings by the Lehmann Quintet. Now we wanted to see the place for ourselves.' His eyes were pleading with us as he spoke.

'But Ruediger Lehmann died many years ago.' I replied quickly before his widow could say anything.

'But the spirit, the spirit, young lady is all around in this room.' His face lit up when he said it. 'Karl Paekel, it is an honour to meet you, Fraulein ....?'

'Hilde, just call me Hilde.'

'Fraulein Hilde, it is.' With that he took charge of the wheelchair, expertly pushing it to the back of the café to our table. 'I believe this has been reserved for you. Madam, I am sorry for the intrusion.' He nodded at Frau Lehmann and returned to his friends.

'Do you know what uniform that is?' I asked the owner when he came over with our usual order of pots of coffee and freshly baked cake.

'Huntsmen, an Infantry Division, based just outside the town.' He realised that it did not mean anything to us and continued. 'Huntsmen have been a long proud tradition with Goslar.'

It rained when we left the café. Karl must have watched us all the time. There he was again. 'Fraulein Hilde, I will get a car. Just wait here. 'With that he disappeared through the door.

He helped Frau Lehmann into the front passenger seat of the jeep, took the wheelchair and loaded it onto the back. I sat behind him. It took only a few minutes to get to our apartment and once we were there Frau Lehmann asked him to come inside.

Chapter 12

I loved the mountains. I loved the smell of the pine trees. I loved collecting pine cones for the stove in the sitting room. I loved the cool moss under my bare feet. I loved Goslar with its magnificent building, quaint houses, spiky towers, Market Square. I loved the cafés, but most of all I loved Karl.

Karl loved taking photographs. Frau Lehmann gave him her late husband's Kodak Brownie and now we took pictures of everywhere and everything. There was a studio which could develop them for us in town. The photographer there was a close friend of Frau Lehmann and we only had to pay for the paper and the chemicals. I was sending photos back to my mother to share with my brothers and sisters. In return I was rewarded with letters from home. Most of them from Erika and she let our little sisters decorate them with kisses. In the evening I would sit in front of Frau Lehmann's armchair. She had insisted some months ago that I call her Charlotte, which I only did when we were alone. We would look at the latest photograph. I used to tease her with my 'Guess where that was taken' questions, and eight times out of ten she could name the exact spot. Like me, she had made Goslar and the Harz Mountains her choice of home. When she was in too much pain to play the game I would read to her. She loved me to read poems written by Goethe and Schiller.

But she also had books by many writers whose work had been publicly burned in Berlin during the rampage in May 1933. Books from Carl Zuckmeyer and Hermann Hesse and many others. These books were not displayed in the big cupboard with the glass doors in the living room. I knew the hiding place was under the wooden floorboards in her bedroom and when she felt especially low and vulnerable she asked me to get them for her. But not before I had checked that the flat was empty, all the doors securely looked and the curtains drawn. And even then, it sounded like a mere whisper when I read them to her. She made me promise not to talk to Karl about these evenings and she knew I would keep my word.

On other nights we would listen to gramophone recordings of the Berlin Philharmonic or songs written by Heinrich Heine and composed by Robert Schumann or Franz Schubert.

What I did not love was going out and leaving Frau Lehmann behind.

'Hilde, go have a good time, I will be fine. I don't know why you fuss.' If she had the physical strength to push me out through the front door, I suppose she would have done so. I always made sure the cook would be at home whilst I was away. But still in my sub-consciousness I had an uneasy feeling every time the latch clicked shut when I left.

Karl took me to the *Hotel Achterman,* which was right in the Square and was favoured by many young officers and their lady friends. In the afternoon there were tea dances and it was often difficult to find a table. We were laughing and joking with some of Karl's fellow Officers when the cook stormed into the café. 'Hilde! You have to come back!' I looked for my coat and could not find it straight away. It was hidden under several layers of jackets which I pulled off and dropped on the floor, all the while apologising. Karl and the cook waited for me outside. The walk, which would normally take about fifteen minutes, took us about five, but it seemed to take forever. Out of breath the cook tried to explain to us what had happened. All we could make out was that Frau Lehmann had had a visit from the Gestapo.

Frau Lehmann was lying on the living room floor in front of her chair when we got there. She had tried to get up to confront the two uniformed men invading her house. Her muscular sclerosis had become much worse in the three and half years I had been here and she found it more difficult to move every day. But still her pride would not let her take any intrusion sitting down. Photographs were scattered all around. Karl and I saw at once that these were pictures we had taken.

41

'Charlotte.' I called her name, bent down and stroked her head. Karl looked at me in surprise when I used her first name, but let it pass.

'I am fine, just help me up.' She tried to give me a reassuring smile, which was not very convincing. Karl lifted her up gently and only now I realised how frail she looked. She was almost like a little girl in Karl's arms.

The cook brought us hot, black, sweet tea with a shot of dark rum, which we thankfully accepted and Frau Lehmann got some colour back into her face.

'They raided the photographic studio in town but luckily Jacob was not there, but they did take his address book and some photographs. Now they are doing searches at all the addresses.' She was still shaking when she told us. Karl had picked up our innocent photographs and scrutinised every one very closely.

'Did they search your apartment?' I asked, not looking at Karl.

'No, one of them recognised me, he knew my husband. He made sure they left after a few minutes.'

'Charlotte.' I purposefully used her first name now. 'You must leave, do you have anywhere else you could go?'

'My younger sister lives in Switzerland and has asked me many times to come and live with her and her husband. They live in *Basle* and he has a dentist practise.' Her head was slightly bent down when she said it, as if she did not want to look at me.

'Good, that is what we are going to do. We will arrange for you to move and live there. *Basle* sounds a wonderful place and it is a good solution.' I held her hand whilst I tried to sound like I did not have a care in the world.

'And you, Hilde, what about you? Will you come with me?' She had her mischievous smile again as she asked me.

But before I could reply Karl said: 'My Garrison is being moved out to *Hildesheim*. I was going to tell you today and I wanted to ask you to come with me.' He was still clutching the photos when he spoke.

'Karl, where is *Hildesheim?*' was all I could reply.

Chapter 13

1936 Christmas Eve
Hildesheim, Lower Saxony

Christmas Eve has always been magical for me. I was far from home and wanted to make my family in East Prussia part of my Christmas Celebrations. I took some coffee cups from the cabinet, turned them upside down, placed them on the window sill in the kitchen, lit small white candles and let the wax drip onto the back of the cups. Once there was enough wax to make the candles stick I pressed them down and held them until they were firmly in place. I continued slowly making sure they would not topple over and lit one for my parents, one for my brothers, one for my sisters and a special one, which had little gold stars on them, for Erika.

My new flat in Einumer Strasse number 60, Hildesheim, was on the ground floor. Normally I had a good view from the kitchen and could spot people arriving from some distance. The kitchen was cold today and the window was frozen from the inside. I had to blow on it and then quickly rub it with my sleeve before it could freeze over again. I was waiting for Karl who had hoped to find a small Christmas tree which we wanted to decorate together. His Garrison was stationed in barracks only about a 10 minute walk away and I had found work there in the Officers' Mess.

The parcel I received from my mother was on the kitchen table, we would open it tonight in the candle light from the tree. I managed to find a stand and some silver coloured lametta and small red baubles at the corner shop. Frau Bucker, who lived above me, had given me a radio and some furniture which used to belong to her mother who had recently died.

I was worried how Karl would react to my news, I had to tell him soon and chose tonight of all nights. My heart missed a beat and my

43

breathing increased when I spotted Karl making his way through the snow and, yes, he was carrying a tree.

I hurried to the front door and let him in. He leaned the tree against the wall in the hall, took off his coat and shook the snowflakes off before he lifted me up and swung me around. 'I love you, Fraulein Hilde.' This little ritual had become part of our lives.

'Karl, we are going to have a baby.' There, I had said it, I would not have found the courage to tell him later. Karl let go of me, stumbled backwards and his face drained of all colour.

'But how?' he stopped in mid-sentence, took a step towards me, held me tight, turned round, got his coat, walked out of the door and closed it behind him. I could hear the snow crunching beneath his feet as he walked away.

I don't know how long I stood there staring at the closed door in front of me, unable to move. But eventually, like an automaton, I took the tree into the living room and tried to put it in the holder. Then I just sat there. I thought about my father always just sitting and staring into space without any reaction to what was going on around him. I was brought out of my shock by a loud banging from the front door.

Through the glass I could see slightly blurred dark figures and when I opened it there was Karl with two of his friends. One of them had a grey blanket over his shoulder, the other a big box of wood and Karl had two boxes piled on top of each other.

'Hilde, what is the matter? Let us in.' He looked back nervously when he said it.

'We believe congratulations are in order, Fraulein Hilde,' said one of his friends.

'But I thought ...' I stammered. 'You thought what?' asked Karl pushing past me into the kitchen. 'I thought you had left me.'

'Left you, and miss the birth of our first child, whatever made you think that? Come here Fraulein Hilde.' He put his arms around me and held me close.

One of his friends made the fire in the kitchen stove. Karl laid out all the food they had brought from the Officer's Mess. There was a goose, red cabbage potato salad, Frankfurter sausages, bread, milk, butter and real coffee. His fellow officers fixed the tree, lit the fire in the sitting room, left the blanket full of coal in the hall and said their goodbyes.

'Happy Christmas, Fraulein Hilde. Karl, we will cover your watch tomorrow. Happy Christmas.' They saluted and left.

That Christmas Eve we sat on cushions on the floor in front of the warm sitting room stove, eating our potato salad and hot Frankfurters with delicious mustard.

Chapter 14

I knew from the first time I met her, that I was not good enough for her son. Karl's mother's face said it all. She looked at me with contempt and kept staring at my, by now, bulging waistline.

We had come to *Holzminden* to invite his parents and his sister to our wedding which was to be in two weeks, the 27th March 1937. She made it clear to me that I had obviously tricked her son and was now going to trap him into a loveless marriage. When Karl and his father went outside to check on the horses, his mother offered me some money to call it off and to go back to East Prussia to live with my parents and raise my child.

I did not tell Karl what his mother suggested but on our way home to Hildesheim I expressed my doubt that they would be at the wedding ceremony.

I had been back to Tilsit twice over the last two months to get the required paperwork. I needed proof of being from Aryan descent before I could marry an Officer. My parents' Birth Certificates and Marriage Licence were kept in a large chest in the main bedroom, but to find information about my Grandfather proved more difficult. My Grandmother died when my father was six years old and my Grandfather had never been able to read and write, hardly ever worked and totally neglected his children. The local Squire took pity on my father. He let him come and live with him and sent him to the local school together with his own children. In turn my father had helped on his farm.

I enlisted Erika's help, gave her all the information I had, the town she had to travel to, the farm where my father worked as a young man, the address of the school and Town Hall.

Erika, fourteen years old, was amazing. On my second visit she proudly presented the papers together with my application form. I was so thankful I took her with me everywhere I went and by the time I got my Certificate, she knew the Officers and personnel as much as I did. I was astonished at her skill, the way she grasped situations and the way she could charm the sternest clerk.

Frau Bucker, my lovely neighbour , how would I have coped without her help. She not only found some white material for a dress, she made it for me. I did not realise until then that she was an accomplished seamstress. She had made dresses in the past for the department store here in town, but now only made clothes for family and friends. On my last visit to Tilsit I took the dresses for Gisela, Traute and Grete with me, but I wanted to wait with Erika's dress until the last minute. The only material we could find for my little sisters had been light blue twill, but Frau Buecker worked her magic, made long sleeved dresses, with two large pockets below the waist. Each dress had a different coloured lace collar with flower shaped buttons on the cuffs and pockets matching the collar.

I hoped Oleg got my letter and he and Ludmilla would be able to travel. They had been married for 3 years now and had a little girl.

My family had yet to meet Karl and I prayed that he would get a better reception from my father, than I got from Karl's mother. There was no doubt in my mind, that the rest of the family would like him instantly.

He arrived two days before the actual ceremony. My aunt had changed her front room into a bedroom. Karl was to stay there until we were married and we both stayed there for a couple of days afterwards.

The river was still frozen solid and the wind from the east cut through your clothes like pins sticking into one of those small cushions in Frau Bucker's sewing kit. Karl and I walked into the church together, navigating pieces of icicles recently fallen from the church roof. My parents were inside with our guests, my aunts and uncles, cousins and some of my friends from school. My brothers and sisters waited for me at the door. Erika held Traute's hand. I was totally overwhelmed when I looked at them all. Erika had plaited her little sister's hair with inter-woven ribbons, matching the colour of the trim on the dresses. She had done the same to her hair but used all of the three different colours which set of her soft lilac dress beautifully. I started to cry when I saw them.

Oleg stepped out from behind the door with his usual grin handing me a bunch of white lilacs. He had remembered how much I liked them and I had no idea where he got them from at this time of the year. All I could say to Karl was, 'Did you know that Oleg would be here?'

'And there is Ludmilla' he answered. 'I met them yesterday.'

I pinched his arm and gave him my, 'Why did you not tell me?' look.

He just shrugged his shoulders. 'Fraulein Hilde, is this how you are supposed to treat your soon-to-be-husband?'

There was nobody at our wedding from Karl's family, he did not seem very concerned but I felt truly sorry for him. We did, however, accept the money which we had been sent and now we could get some of the things we needed for our first child.

My sister, Lisbet, was there with her husband. I did not even know I had a sister Lisbet. Apparently she was almost eight years older than me and the story I was now told was that my mother had been very ill when Lisbet was born and a distant relative had looked after her and moved away. It was only a year ago when my mother found out where she was living.

My father was very quiet most of the day, but he had hired the church hall and we had food delivered from the train company's canteen. All the drinks had been arranged and paid for by Karl's fellow Officers and arrived from the local Garrison. When my father finally felt in the mood to speak with Karl, he had already had a few of those drinks and spilled some beer over Karl's pristine uniform. Karl just hugged him and together they laughed, but he did glance back at me, with a face which said, 'It's alright, we will worry about the uniform later.'

Ludmilla was as pretty in reality, as she was on the photograph they had sent to me and I felt immediately drawn to her. Her German was excellent and she told me she was already teaching it to her young daughter. I introduced them to my mother and when they were out of sight I said to her, 'Mother, you know Oleg and Ludmilla over there?' My mother turned round. 'Yes, your friends.'

'Please promise me, if Oleg, Ludmilla and their children, ever come to you, it would be because I have sent them. Promise me, you will take them in.'

Now my mother took another look. 'But, why?'

'Mother, just promise me, regardless of what father would say. Please.'

Finally my mother looked straight into my eyes. 'I promise you, Hilde, I will not turn them away.'

Out of the corner of my eye I could see Erika holding her first glass of wine and coming over to where we were standing.

'Hilde, I am leaving school in six weeks, can I come and live with you? I can help you in the house and look after your baby.'

I put my arm around my mother's shoulder, gave her a quick squeeze with my finger nails.

'Too late, Erika' I laughed, 'You have got an apprenticeship in our Town Hall. It's your fault really, for charming the senior clerk.'

Chapter 15

Summer 1937
Hildesheim

Just after Klaus was born my mother came to stay with us.

Karl had arranged that she could join a military convoy from *Tilsit* to Berlin. The Garrison in my home town, which had been empty for many years, had been re-commissioned by the Wehrmacht. The only train running for the civilian population was now once a week, all the others had been taken over for military purposes and their personnel.

Once my mother reached Berlin she stayed with Helene and Frank for a few days and then continued to travel by train to Hannover. It was a slow journey with stops at every town and village, but at least my mother did not have to change anywhere and wait for a connection .A young soldier had given up his seat and after she proudly told him that her son-in-law was an Officer, he had kept a watchful eye on her throughout the trip.

Karl picked her up at Hannover Station in an open jeep. I never believed my mother had so much adventure within her.

It was the very first time I had my mother all for myself and I relished her attention. I was very keen to impress her and gain her approval, but I did not need to have worried. My mother loved every minute we spent together. My long-lost sister Lisbet was back, living at home. I was beginning to understand how my mother must have suffered every day she had spent parted from her child, hoping she would walk through the door, fearing she would never see her again. It must have been unbearable, especially since the first moment I set eyes on Lisbet it was like I was looking into a mirror. We both had green eyes, our heights seemed identical and both of our hair colours were light auburn with a few highlights. Very much like our mother, whereas all my brothers and sisters were blond, resembling our father.

We took Klaus in the pram with us most days. We walked the narrow winding roads, we marvelled at the half -timbered buildings, most of them decorated with colourful carvings. We visited the churches and of course Hildesheim's main attraction the 1000 year old Rosebush at the Cathedral. Legend told us, as long as the Rosebush flourishes, Hildesheim will not decline.

The day we walked up the *Galgenberg,* a mountainous area which is the foothills of the Harz Mountains, we left Klaus with Inge. Inge had been assigned to us during the previous month. Young women were now required to spend, as part of their education program, some of their time in a family's household, as the boys were encouraged to join the Hitler Youth.

We took a picnic with us which I carried in my old trusted rucksack. We ate our sandwiches of rye bread with salami and cheese which my mother had brought all the way from *Tilsit.* We had a flask with cold tea. Plus biscuits, which my mother had baked the day before.

I had placed the blanket on the grass in front of the tower. Wild daisies were all around us. From where we sat the hill sloped slightly down - this was a good place to toboggan in the winter, so I had been told. I hoped my mother would have enough energy to climb to the top of the tower which for some time now had become my favourite place to visit. I had even carried Klaus up here not long after he was born. I explained to him everything he would be able to recognise one day. I was like an Empress showing her heir the land which would become his Kingdom.

From there you could see as far as thirty kilometres. Below us, the whole town spread out in front of you. If you looked north you could see our street and over the rooftops the green copper spires of the churches. You turned to the west and you saw the factories surrounded by woodland. To the south you saw the hospitals, but to the east you could clearly see the Harz Mountain with its highest peak the '*Brocken*' and there in the distance, nestled in the centre of the hills, was Goslar. I came up here when I felt sad, sometimes Karl and I came together, we would hold hands, silently trying to figure out Goslar's exact location.

My mother did not complain about the steps but was a little bit nervous when she realised the last staircase was made from metal, round like a helter-skelter and, worse, you could see right to the bottom. I took her hand and instantly felt she knew how important it was for me that we went up these steps together.

At the top I spread out my arms turned round and round and shouted 'Hello! Hello!'

'ello, ello' it echoed back.

'Come on mother, you try it.' I coaxed her. 'Oh no, Hilde, I could not possibly.' She looked embarrassed.

'Yes you must, let's do it together. On the count of three, two turns, arms open wide and shout as loud as you can. 'One, two ...... two and a half, three.'

'Hello! Hello!' 'ello, ello lo, lo,' was the reply. We looked at each other and burst out laughing. We laughed so much I had to hold on to my sides. I had never before heard my mother laugh like this.

Chapter 16

9th of November 1938

9th of November 1938
Hildesheim

Fierce banging against the apartment door woke me from a deep sleep. Little Klaus, one and a half years old, talking and walking, his energy had taken its toll on me today. That and the fact that I was expecting our second child in just over one month's time. I hoped the knocking was not real and I could get back to sleep. I pulled the duvet closer around me trying not to disturb Karl. It had become very cold during the last week.

The banging continued more persistently and was accompanied by people shouting. I had to get Karl up now and hoped that the noise would not wake Klaus.

'Karl, we have to get up, there is somebody at the door, it sounds urgent.' I muttered and Karl did not hear a word I said. 'Karl, wake up, there is somebody at the door.' This time I shook him. He jumped up and immediately was fully alert. He grabbed his trousers and went into the hall. He had left the bedroom door slightly ajar, I was unsure whether it was deliberately, but I could hear some of what was being said.

There must have been several people and most of them talking at once. 'Sir, there are riots going on in town,' is what I could make out. I got out of bed, the duvet still round me and took a peek through the opening at the hinge side of the door. I saw three men entering the hall. Karl must have heard me and looked round. After that, the voices got quiet and all three men looked at my door. Karl turned round and came back into the room.

'Karl, what is going on, tell me?'

'I have to get dressed and go with my fellow Officers.'

'Karl, they are not in uniform. Talk to me!' I started to sound hysterical.

'Sir, are you on duty?' one of them asked from the hall.

'No, not right now, not until the day after tomorrow.' Karl replied, looking at me. I got his message, that he also had no idea what was happening and where they wanted him to go.

'Sir, please do not wear your uniform, we have not told anybody that we are going to check on what is happening in the town.'

'Karl, please „...' I started to say.

'Hilde, these are my comrades, I have got to go with them. There are riots and lootings in the Town Square. As far as they know the apartment store, Rosenberg's shoe shop, Neuberger's toy shops and others have been destroyed.'

'Karl, these shops are owned by ....' before I could finish my sentence he interrupted.

'Yes, I know, and the Synagogue is burning.' His face was as white as a sheet.

'No! You are not leaving me here. I am coming with you.' I started to get my clothes at the same time as Klaus started crying.

'Hilde, now you are being unreasonable. You can't come. I will get Frau Bucker so she can stay with you. If you want to do something, please try and find a radio station with proper information.' He looked back and whispered, 'not the usual propaganda and keep the sound low.'

'Karl, please be careful.' I pulled him back into the room and put one arm around him, holding Klaus with the other. 'I love you, Herr Paekel.' I blew a kiss onto his ear.

'I love you, Fraulein Hilde.' I felt his soft touch on my lips and smiled, he still called me Fraulein Hilde.

Frau Bucker was in her nightdress and dressing gown when she came downstairs but she had quickly found some clothes and shoes before she left her apartment. Whilst she got changed I dressed Klaus who was totally bewildered and thought it was a game. He pointed to the window and said 'dark, Klaus play.' 'Yes Sweetheart, you go to Frau Bucker while Mamma gets dressed.'

The three of us went into the sitting room and we lit a new fire trying to get warm as we tried to wake up. I went to the radio to find out what was going on. Another knock on the door but not that loud and a small voice 'Hilde, are you up?'

I ran to open it and there was Maria with her little boy Hugo. 'Oh my God!' she said. She saw my blank look. 'Have you not heard?' she asked.

'Heard what?' Mr Bucker and I said together.

'They are attacking all the shops and homes owned by the Jewish population, ransacking everything in sight, setting the Synagogues alight.'

'Who?'

'The SS.'

'What, here in Hildesheim?' I asked.

'No, everywhere.' Maria replied.

'Everywhere? How do you know?'

Maria explained that her husband Egon, who was a doctor at the local hospital, got a phone call to come to work straight away, all off duty personnel had to report immediately. Egon never liked to be ordered around and had no intention of going until he was told exactly why.

'Let's hear what we are told on the radio.' I went over and turned it on. After a few turns of the dial we heard the announcement:

'Unidentified Youth have taken it upon themselves to damage Jewish shops, homes and Synagogues in an apparent revenge for the assassination of Ernst von Rath in Paris by the Polish Jew Herschal Grynszpan. This was an unprovoked murder of a German Diplomat. We urge our good German citizens to remain calm and stay indoors. Order will be restored as soon as possible.'

'Unidentified Youth! Maybe their SS uniform would help to identify them.' Frau Bucker said sarcastically.

'Wait and let's see whether we can get any other information.' Maria was turning the station selector on the radio again, pressing her ear as close to the speaker as she could.

'Here, this is the one. she said.

'But it is in English?' questioned Frau Bucker.

'Maria is from Belgium and is fluent in French and English' I explained. Maria translated the BBC broadcast:

'Organized Nazi activists, together with sympathisers, are staging a nationwide attack on stores and homes owned by the Jewish community. Houses are ransacked, stores destroyed and looted.

Synagogues throughout the country are burning. Meanwhile the German Authorities are standing by and are doing nothing to prevent this atrocity. We have heard of the arrests of Jewish people trying to defend their property. Several Jewish people have been reported killed. Stay tuned and we will bring you updates every hour.'

We sat in stunned silence looking at Klaus and Hugo playing on the floor with a wooden horse and truck bought at Neuberger's toy shop only a few days ago. Frau Neuberger always lets our boys play with some old toys while we look around and if she has toys which have a small mark or some paint missing, most of the time she includes one for free with our other purchases.

It was starting to get light outside and the News on the radio had not changed. We were not given any further information. Maria went outside and walked to the other side of the road. From there she could see the smoke of the burning buildings. We watched her through the kitchen window and she looked back at us with a sombre expression.

We made some coffee and had some breakfast. Frau Bucker helped me to feed the boys while Maria went home to leave a message for Egon in case he got home and worried about their whereabouts. I had not heard from Karl and I was becoming increasingly anxious.

About mid-morning we could not stand the uncertainty any longer. We had to go and see for ourselves. We had to pass the Railway Station before we reached the town centre. Long queues of people waited outside the station. Women and children with bags and suitcases huddled together. Maria spotted a nurse working at the hospital and rushed over, only to be stopped by a pimply young man in a Hitler Youth Uniform. I knew him and shouted: 'Friedbert, if you think I will not tell your mother what you are up to, you are wrong.' His face went bright red and he let Maria pass.

The nurse told Maria that they are leaving for Holland to take a ferry to England. She also said that the SS had arrested most men, including her husband. Egon had given her Maria's brother's address in Brussels and she would get a message to him with her

English contact. She had enough time to tell Maria a couple of code words to be used before she was allowed onto the platform.

Walking into the town centre was like walking on an ice skating rink. Most shop fronts had been smashed in, sledgehammers were still lying in front doors. The pavement and streets were covered with broken glass. Frau Neuberger was outside her shop. The windows broken and the shelves stripped bare. As if in a trance she was brushing the glass from one side to the other and back again. We went over and offered to help her but Frau Neuberger looked at us with such contempt, as if she had never seen us before and she certainly did not ever want to see us again.

We could not bring ourselves to walk to the synagogue.

Chapter 17

Maria and I first met at the hospital. We were in the same ward having our first child. We took to each other straight away. It was instant friendship. Best of all we soon found out we only lived one street away from each other. Maria had moved to Hildesheim from Belgium two years before me. She had met Egon in Brussels where he had attended an International Medical Conference. She had worked at the reception of the hotel he stayed at. Egon was a widower and about ten years older than Maria. They married after a whirlwind romance and Maria moved to Hildesheim. Before Hugo was born they lived in a one-bedroom apartment in the town centre and she said they were lucky to find the place they had now.

'That's about all there is to it.' She used to say to me. With Maria, there was nothing like 'all there is to it' of course. Maria was as colourful as she was big. She was bubbly, she did not seem to be afraid of anything, would always voice her opinion (which worried me no end) and had an infectious laugh. Maria could find a solution to most things, however challenging. If you had Maria as your friend or Maria was nearby, you felt safe.

Egon's colleagues said that Maria had been a breath of fresh air for Egon, whereas before he was formal and stiff, now he was entertaining and adventurous. Maria dabbled with a bit of fortune-telling on the side. On evenings when we were alone she would bring her cards and tell me what life held in store for me.

Maria and Egon had a telephone installed. He needed it for his calls from and to the hospitals. Egon and Maria let me use it to phone Erika at work and sometimes Frank at the school in Berlin.

In turn I often cooked their favourite meals. Egon used to laugh when he said: 'Hilde, you can phone day and night. Just please do not stop cooking.'

I phoned Frank's school the morning after the burning of the Synagogues and the looting of the stores and houses. He was not there, so I left a message with one of his colleagues that I would be phoning back at lunchtime. Then I phoned Erika but it just rang and rang and rang. I would have to try again.

I spoke to Frank later during the day and what he said was disturbing. He was careful in what he said, making sure he was not overheard. From what I could make out it was a similar situation in Berlin, but only more so since there was a very large Jewish community.

The Synagogue in the *Fasanenstrasse*, which was very close to where Helene and Frank lived, was totally destroyed and the fire was still smouldering.

I tried to get across to him to go to Harel's café, hoping he would understand that I wanted him to go there and check on my friends. I said 'I love Berlin, I still miss it, I used to go to a little café at the Alexander Platz. It is Helene's birthday soon, if the weather is nice why don't you two go there this weekend? She will love it, all the cakes will remind her of home.'

'That's a great idea, a little walk will do her good. She has been a little down lately, our two little monsters are driving her mad. I will tell her you rang, speak to you next week.' With that he hung up.

I did not reach Erika until three days later. Their office had been closed. Most of her Jewish colleagues had left the town and a clean-up operation had begun. That was all she could tell me, but I judged from her voice, that she sounded in shock and decided not to press her any more about it.

Frank phoned Maria the following week and gave her a number I could phone him back on. When I reached him there he told me Harel and his family had been deported back to Poland the day before the burning of the synagogues. All Polish-speaking people in possession of a Polish pass were required to report to the nearest police station. They were then allowed to collect a few possessions, were loaded like cattle onto lorries and trains for their journey back to Poland. That was all the information he could get. Yes, Harel's café and apartment had been completely destroyed.

Chapter 18

Karl received notice to report to the 1st Light Brigade in Erfurt. We had known for some time that his position in Hildesheim was only temporary. Still, it came as a shock. I adored having Karl around most days and the children loved it when their father was at home. He was never too tired to play with them. Klaus used to 'ride' on his back, whilst Karl was crawling on all fours through the apartment. 'Hop, hop horsey' he would be shouting and kicking Karl in his ribs with both heels, just as he had watched his father on parade.

It was Klaus's second birthday tomorrow and we had made plans. We wanted to go out again and had asked Egon, Maria and Hugo to come with us to the lake. It had been lovely and warm since April and the weather in June 1939 was just perfect. We had taken the children on several trips there already. Klaus running in and out of the shallow water and Renate, now six months old, playing but never venturing from the safety of her blanket.

Renate made me smile every time I looked at her. Whereas Klaus was blond and robust, Renate was tiny and delicate. She had dark chestnut-coloured hair and lots of it. People used to stare at her when she was sitting in her pram. Her skin was like porcelain and we called her 'our Little Snow White.'

'You still go with everybody, we can't disappoint them.' Karl tried to act like there was nothing to it, him going to be about 180 km away from us and not knowing when he would be coming back. 'Maria and Hugo have a telephone, I will be able to call.'

'Karl, I am going over to Maria, I will not be long. I have just put Renate to bed, don't let Klaus make too much noise. I will be back in about an hour.' I kissed him but he looked at me with a puzzled expression.

'I will explain to her about tomorrow, there will be plenty of time for Maria, me and the children to go out when you have gone.' I said.

Maria was surprised to see me. 'Hilde, that's great, I was just ....' she looked at me.

'What happened?'

'You tell me, you are supposed to be the clairvoyant here.' I replied sullenly.

'Ouch!' was all she said. But I saw the hurt in her face.

'Come on, tell me, something has happened, am I right?' she gave me her reassuring smile.

'Karl has been deployed. He is to report to Erfurt.' I could not stop my tears any longer.

'Maria, I am so worried, I have a bad feeling about it.' She came closer and put her arms around me.

'Oh, Hilde, I wish I could find the right words to comfort you. Please be brave, he might not be there that long.'

That did make me smile a little. 'Thank you, that's exactly why I am so afraid. You and me, we both have seen the propaganda Goebbels wants us to believe. Last time we went to the Cinema, we almost walked out. We only stayed in case somebody might recognise us. If what they showed us is only half true, it is terrifying. We both know Hitler will not give up.'

I counted myself lucky to have Inge. She had agreed to look after the three children that afternoon when Maria and I wanted to go to see a movie. It was a light-hearted musical revue called *The Stars Shine* and when we got there we were surprised to see a long queue.

Like almost everybody else in town, we wanted to get out and be entertained for a few hours. We managed to get two seats together, at the front of the cinema. We did expect a News reel but instead were presented with Goebbels propaganda show *Words and Deeds* -a ten minute documentary showing the economic progress of Germany under Hitler.

We were sitting not far from the screen and had to stare at Goebbels and Hitler's faces close up.

It sent shivers down our spine when people cheered and applauded. The audience actually believed what they were being fed.

Maria kept pushing me in my side, indicating with her head we should leave but I stayed frozen in my seat, too afraid to make a move, in case I got lynched on the way out.

To make matters worse, this re- make of the original film had undertones of the, by now usual, propaganda throughout. We will not return to the cinema for a long time, that is what we promised ourselves on the way home.

Karl packed and left on Klaus's birthday. Lucky Klaus was too young to understand. But I can still hear his little voice when he clung to his father and said: 'Pappa, come home.'

Chapter 19

'But I don't understand. Why? Why are you being trained for Tank Warfare?' The telephone line was not very clear and it had a lot of crackling and background noise. Maybe I had misheard altogether. 'Where are you anyway?' I had to shout and hoped Maria's neighbours did not do their usual and press a glass against the wall so that they could hear better.

'We left Erfurt last week and are now further East.' I could barely make it out. He either really did not know exactly where he was or he could not tell me.

'Karl, have you been told when you can come home? We have not seen you once since you left and it is already the middle of August.' Click and we were cut off.

'Karl! Karl! Can you hear me, Karl? It is no use Maria, the line went dead.'

'What did he say?' she asked.

I let out a long sigh. 'He is being instructed in Tank Warfare. Maria, the more I hear about it the less I like it. Why on earth train him in Tank Warfare? He was part of the Cavalry. And why have they gone further East? You are sure we understood correctly? There is an agreement that if Hitler did get what he was after, the Sudetenland , he promised in return, there would be no further attacks and we would have peace.'

'Yes, that is the way we heard it.' Maria nodded.

'Did we get this from the usual propaganda machine, or did you hear that on the BBC?'

We heard a noise next door. Maria put a finger on her lips to indicate to be quiet.

'Yes, we know you are there Frau Meyer, why don't you just knock on the door, saves straining your ears!' I shouted as loud as I could, my lips almost touching the wall, in sheer frustration.

The children who until then had been happily playing on the floor with some wooden clothes pegs, all looked round together and started crying.

'Mamma!' Klaus came running and I saw a wet patch on Maria's pride and joy carpet.

'Come here, Klaus.' I folded my arms around him. 'I am so sorry Maria. The children have never heard me shout. I frightened them.'

Maria had already picked up Hugo. We looked at each other and burst out laughing. When we got our breath back, Maria said: 'We really must be more careful and it was on the BBC anyway. That plus Hitler and Stalin had just signed a non-aggression pact.'

Chapter 20

1st September 1939

1st September 1939

We all sat around the radio in my living room. Egon, Maria, Frau Bucker, Inge and myself. We held the children very close. Renate was trying to wiggle out of my grasp but I could not bear to let her out of my reach for even one second. Now our children needed our protection more than ever.

At around five in the morning there were blaring sirens throughout the town. The shrill noise was still ringing in our ears. Frau Bucker got here first followed by Egon and Maria. Inge had stayed overnight.

Even Egon and the ever-optimistic Maria seemed lost for words. At the beginning we all talked at once.

'What do you think this means?'

'Do you think Hitler has attacked Poland after all?'

'But he promised he wouldn't.' All faces turned to young innocent Inge. If she believed Hitler, we knew loads of others would too.

'Inge, do you think you could make us some coffee, and there are a few slices of cake left from yesterday, I think we could all do with something right now. I will help you in a minute.' Frau Bucker had grasped the situation immediately. After Inge left the room she continued, 'we can't involve Inge, she might not realise any remark from her could put us all in danger. We will have our coffee and maybe then she should go. Hilde. you should tell her to check on her family. Meanwhile let's not speculate until we can talk freely.'

We all nodded in agreement.

'In any case,' said Egon, 'we can put the radio on and maybe they will give us some information.' This he said with sarcastic undertones.

'Ok but only the official stations, agreed?' 'Agreed' we all said.
Frau Bucker went to join Inge in the kitchen to fetch the cups and saucers and small plates. We waited for any radio broadcast until Inge had also sat down. Egon turned the sound up so we could all hear.

Goebbels' voice bellowed the official party line from the speaker:

'My Good German Citizens. Yesterday Polish soldiers staged an attack , pilfered, raided homes and murdered your fellow Countrymen. They slaughtered innocent men, women and children. Our Fuehrer had no option but to retaliate and defend our Fatherland and its People. Our thoughts are with our brave troops and we all hope for a speedy resolve of this grave matter. Heil Hitler.'

'You see' said Inge, 'we were attacked and Hitler is only defending us. Minister Goebbels said it would be resolved soon.'

'Yes, so he did, Inge, you are right. I think maybe soon you should check on your family. It is best not to send your brothers and sisters to school today, what do you think?'

The words just tumbled out of me. I hoped she did not pick up on how urgently I wanted her to leave.

'Do you think I could go, will you be alright?' She looked at me.

'Yes, yes, I will be just fine. Maybe you can come back in the afternoon. But there is really no need.' I added quickly. 'Here, have some coffee and cake, you must be as tired as we all are.'

We made polite, light-hearted noises for another 20 minutes and I finally closed the door behind her.

'Has she gone?' I nodded a yes. 'Now let's hear the other version.' Egon twiddled with the dial until we heard the BBC. It took a while until Egon and Maria translated, one interrupting the other to make sure we got what they heard as best as they could tell us. The BBC broadcast had said:

'Just before dawn today, German tanks, infantry and cavalry penetrated Polish territory on several fronts with 5 armies, a total of 1.5 million troops. German planes are bombarding cities. Communications have been broken but earlier reports say that German planes were attacking in squadrons of 50 every half hour. The Polish town of Danzig has declared itself as part of the Third

66

Reich. There is heavy fighting reported along the whole of the East Prussian border. These unprovoked attacks follow yesterday's reports on the German radio that the border town of Gliwice had been raided by a group of Polish soldiers. This, however, cannot be confirmed.'

'Hilde!' Maria shouted. 'Do you feel .....' That was all I could hear. Renate tumbled onto the floor, I rushed out and reached the bathroom just in time.

Egon had followed me and held my head whilst I was violently sick. Then he sat me on the bathroom floor, took a fresh flannel from the shelf, ran it under the tap and cleaned my face with very cold water. That helped me to recover a little. He then took my pulse and slowly lifted me back onto my feet. Maria rushed forward when she saw us entering the room and helped to lay me flat onto the settee.

'Do you know whether there is any alcohol in the flat?' Egon asked. 'I have a little bit of brandy upstairs.' Frau Bucker volunteered and got up to fetch it. All this was like a blur to me. Renate was still crying from when I let her fall, but a small piece of the cake soon dried her tears and she crawled over to Klaus and Hugo who were now playing with their toy tractors.

The brandy burned my throat but helped to settle my stomach and took the sour taste away. It seemed like a long time but eventually I sat back up.

'Karl told me he went East when we last talked and now we know why. Danzig is close to my hometown and there is fighting all along the of the East Prussian/Polish border. You can't get closer to Poland then Tilsit. Oh my God, my whole family.' I put my head down and covered it with my hands and started sobbing.

'Mamma, Mamma,' Klaus came running over, pushed Maria and Egon out of the way and climbed onto my lap. 'Mamma, no cry, Pappa come home.' I hugged him tight. Not even two and a half years old and already he had understood.

Chapter 21

'I am sorry, the school is closed today. I am the caretaker. Who did you say was calling?' I just hung up. I certainly was not going to leave a message for Frank at his school. I will try again tomorrow. That is, if he was still allowed to teach Geography as we knew it.

'You are right, Maria, the school is closed. What if Frank does not go along with the official 'party line' as they will most certainly be ordered to do, to brainwash their students?'

'Look, Hilde, Frank must decide for himself and he knows how to look after Helene and their children. He will let you know as soon as he can what is happening over there.'

'Still no connection with Erika?' she asked.

'No, but I will keep on trying. And you are sure Karl has not tried to phone in the last few days?' I kept asking her the same questions over and over again.

She shook her head for the third time today.

Earlier on we had made an arrangement to go food shopping. Now I would not leave the children with Inge. I simply could not let them out of my sight. It had been two days since Germany had invaded Poland and there had been no further information as far as we could make out.

We got to *Beuerman's,* our local grocery store, about lunchtime. It had taken me longer to get the children ready, Renate had been fidgeting all night. She did not want to eat and her head felt hot. Egon would have to check her over when he got home later.

Outside the store there was a large crowd gathering. My heart sank. My first thought was there must be a shortage of essential items. Maria took Hugo and Klaus by their hands and stayed with the pram, whilst I tried to push myself further to the front just to see what was going on. From what I could make out, nobody was being served and everybody was silent. Herr Beuerman was in front of the radio.

Ice cold sweat took hold of me. Something else must have happened. I was almost too afraid to ask and looked backwards and turned towards Maria. She gave me an encouraging nod in return. 'Find out what is going on.'

'Excuse me,' I said, 'is there any news?' I asked the person in front of me, a man about my age. I had to look up to see his face and recognised Hans, our postman. Something was different about him and I could not lay my hands on it straight away. Then it struck me, it was his uniform. It was not the post office dark blue with gold coloured buttons. He was wearing dark brown trousers and a light brown shirt. The swastika: red, white and black armband around his sleeve.

Before I had the chance to backtrack he recognised me too. 'Frau Paekel!' he shouted. 'How are you? How are the children and how is your husband?' By now some people had turned round to look at us. 'I, I don't know,' that was all I could think of saying at the moment. And like an idiot I rambled on. 'Don't you work at the Post Office anymore?'

'No, this is where the future is Frau Paekel, you mind my word,' and with that statement he pointed to the swastika on his arm.

'I have to go' I said, 'My children are waiting,' and turned to leave. He followed me, and stroked Klaus over the head. 'Ah, little Klaus. It is little Klaus, that is right, is it not?' He continued. 'And blond, a strong blond boy, how lucky you are.'

'Hans, I really have to go.' I took the pram and shoved my not-so-blond, dark-haired girl under his nose. But not before Maria quickly asked, 'Why is everybody queuing?'

'You have not heard?' Hans smirked, 'Britain and France have declared War on Germany.'

We took our children and moved away. Maria took charge. 'Right,' she said 'we still have to eat something today and the children need to have lunch. What we will do is, walk into town, get some meat and some vegetables and milk if we can. I still have potatoes at home. Then we go to my place and take care of the children. With a bit of luck they might go to sleep for a while. We

69

can listen to the BBC and you, Hilde, can cook for all of us tonight. What do you think?' she asked.

'I think that is a great idea. Also, when Egon comes home I would like him to look at Renate as she does not seem to be very well. Would you mind phoning him at the hospital and ask when he will be home?' I looked hopefully at her when I said it.

Egon had checked Renate several times during the last month and had not found anything wrong with her.

I made a beef goulash, definitely Egon's favourite, but not before I washed Klaus's hair. I can still see Hans' fat fingers touching my precious son. The children ate some of the meat gravy over mashed potatoes and peas mixed together. Again Renate did not eat but I made sure that at least she drank some milk. Maria had some honey which we mixed in.

We then tried to get the BBC News Broadcast but there was a lot of interference on the radio and we started to think that the News Station had been deliberately blocked.

Of course there was more than enough coverage on our official German station.

'Britain and France have made the regrettable decision to jointly declare War on our Country. We now have no option but to defend our fronts to the East, North and West. Troops will be deployed immediately to ensure our borders are safe from any attack. All reserve personnel have to report to their nearest office with the immediate effect. Our thoughts are with our Fuehrer and our brave troops. Heil Hitler.'

Egon was back from work just after five in the afternoon but had to return around midnight. He had heard the same as we had and again tried the BBC, without success. 'What do you think will happen?' I asked Egon and hoped he would re-assure me.

'That mad man will not rest until he has complete supremacy. That is what I think anyway,' he said, followed by 'Any word from Karl?' He could read my answer from the look on my face.

He took Renate's temperature, checked her throat and her pulse. 'I don't know, Hilde, it bothers me that I can't find what the cause is of her being unwell several times in the last few weeks. I would like to take her into the hospital and run some tests.'

'No!' I shouted and picked her up, but was surprised how floppy she felt.

'Can Hilde go with her?' asked Maria. 'I will keep Klaus here and I'll go to Hilde's flat in a minute to pack a few things and tell Inge. Anyway, poor Inge, she will be worried by now why she hasn't heard from us all day.'

Chapter 22

Renate endured two days of tests at the hospital. Inge and I shared sitting by her bedside. She was still very lethargic and slept most of the time. But when she woke up at least she would see one of us. The doctors said that she had a very high white blood cell count and needed to be on a drip. She looked so tiny in her cot.

After two days, Egon accompanied me to see the paediatrician. To my surprise the doctor in charge was a slender woman with slightly grey hair, held back in a bun. She seemed to glide when she elegantly approached us, greeted me and said, 'Frau Paekel, please come in.'

She pointed to a couple of chairs in front of her large desk. Then walked over herself and took a seat behind it. The desk was covered with files and it took a couple of minutes until she found what she was looking for. All the while I fidgeted and feared the worst.

'Ah, yes' she said 'Renate. How old did you say she is? Yes, I can see she is nine month old. Did you say she was crawling?' She looked at Egon who was still wearing his white doctor's overcoat and a stethoscope.

'Sorry, Hilde,' he said. 'I gave as much information as I could think of.'

'Yes' I said, she is crawling. Why?'

'The high white blood count is nothing to worry about, she is fighting an infection. So that is quite normal,' the doctor continued.

'What do you mean, is there something else to worry about?' The doctor seemed to recoil when I shouted.

'Please, Frau Paekel,' she said looking at me and her calmness had a soothing effect. 'Let's just go through our findings, shall we?'

'Renate seems very small for her age, but you have noticed this yourself, right?' I nodded yes to her question.

'We started there and tested her glands. The results have come back. Her pituitary gland is not working properly, it is under-functioning and that is restricting her growth. Also, her thyroid glands are underactive. This could count for her slower than expected development, her tiredness and possible painful muscles, which would explain why she had not started crawling or standing up. That is why I asked the question. I am sorry if I panicked you.' She gave me a soft smile and continued. 'Frau Paekel, I also have children, so I understand how worried you must be.'

I was beginning to recover and asked, 'Is there anything that can be done about it?'

'Yes of course, we found out early which is really good but we have to start her on a course of weekly injections. After two months we will test again. There might be a chance that she will never be of average height but, other than that, with the right medication, everything should settle down. We now know what the problem is and which treatment we can offer. If you have any concern, please come and see me, otherwise I will see you in two months time.' She stood up and we walked to the office door together.

'When can I take Renate home?'

'Maybe at the end of the week. We first want to make sure the infection has cleared up. Egon will let you know.' With that she said her goodbyes.

When I got back home I found a note Maria had left for me on the kitchen table. *Phone Erika,* was all it said.

Chapter 23

I felt sheer relief at finally being able to speak to Erika, although everything she told me filled me with terror.

'Hilde, please come and get me,' she pleaded as soon as she heard my voice. It broke my heart to tell her to slow down. I tried to get an account of what was happening in Tilsit and near the Polish border.

'Erika, you know I can't come and get you. It is too dangerous at the moment for anybody to travel such a long distance by themselves.' I hoped she would forgive me. Of course I wanted her to come, but what I said was also true.

'Erika, please tell me how you are coping. How is everybody in our family? What can you see and what did you hear? I promise you I will try and think of something, alright?' I hoped this promise would help and I racked my brain as to how I could go about it.

'There are soldiers swarming everywhere. We can see the planes from our kitchen window and we can hear the bombs dropping. There is dense smoke all around the town and the smell of burning fires,' she blurted out.

'Hilde? she asked.

'Yes?'

'Do you remember when our cow died when I was little and we had to burn her body? Hilde, it smells like that,' she whispered.

My heart literally froze, I could hardly bear her pain. What comforting words could I find in reply?

'Erika, right now you have to be very brave' was my lame suggestion. 'Tell me how everybody is coping: mother, father and our brothers and sisters.'

'Father is pretending nothing is happening. No, actually now I come to think about it, he says they had it coming for a long time, the Polskis. He is delighted that Danzig has declared itself to be part of Germany. Now, he says, we don't need to travel through Poland to go to Berlin. Not that he has ever been to Berlin, or even knows exactly where it is.' I could hear the resentment in her voice.

'Don't take a lot of notice of what he says, you just be careful what you say to him. Don't forget he lost his arm in the other War and we know how bitter he is about it. Alright?'

'What about mother?' I continued.

'I must say Lisbet is great. She is looking after mother, Gisela, Grete and Traute. She does the cooking and she calms the girls during the bombing. She makes them hide under the beds, which they think is a game. She revels in having found her long-lost family.'

'That is good.' I hoped Erika did not hear my slight tint of jealously. That had been my job to look after my little sisters, and I hardly even knew Lisbet, my elder sister.

'Hilde, she is not you, never is and never will be. Let's just be happy we have her back.' Sixteen years old and already so wise - that was Erika alright!

'Anyway,' she continued, 'That means I don't have to do it and you can come and get me. Right?'

We actually managed to have a little laugh about that. 'Right', I said. 'We can work on it.'

'Oh! No! No!'

'What? What is happening?'

'The planes are coming back. I can hear them approaching but I can't see them yet.'

'Do you have to go into hiding?' I shouted in case she could not hear.

'No, why?' she said 'In any case I am at the office and there are no beds in sight that I could hide under.'

'Who is with you at the office?' I asked her, now worried because we spoke so freely.

'Don't worry, only people I know and trust, plus they are speaking to their own families.'

'What about our brothers?' I wanted to know.

'Well, Arno has disappeared.'

'What do you mean, disappeared?' I asked.

75

'Last year, the day after all the synagogues got burned down, he took some of his things and went. We have not seen or heard from him since.' Erika continued.

'Over a year! He's been missing for over one year? Why did you not tell me before?' I wanted to know.

'I didn't want to worry you and he is old enough to know what he is doing. Also, our father didn't know he had a girlfriend and that she is Jewish.'

'My goodness, Erika, what else did you keep from me?'

'Not much,' she replied.

'Not much, so there is something then?'

'No, not really. Herbert and Helmut are still working hard as ever. And, oh, by the way, I have a boyfriend.' I imagined her little smile, whilst she informed me of her news.

'What! You are far too young to have a boyfriend. Who is he and what does he do?'

'Hilde, please don't be our mother, and no she does not know, and yes he is nice and no to whatever you are thinking and don't worry he is only a friend, alright.'

'By the way' she continued 'I spoke with Frank.'

'You what? When?' I asked this time firmer.

'He rang, apparently could not get hold of you. I just happened to be in the office when the call came. Helene and the children are fine. He was not on the telephone for long. Berlin seems to be in a state of euphoria. He has to attend a rally which will be held at the Olympic Stadium. He could not speak freely but I got the impression that all people, like teachers, government officials, hospital staff and such, have to get their groups together in order to fill the stadium, look enthusiastic and all shout in one voice. The Fuehrer himself will address them.'

'Hilde I have got to go.'

'Please give my love to the family. Also to aunt, uncle and cousins, you hear? Erika, I miss you, I really, really miss you.'

'I miss you too, Hilde. I will be there soon,' and she hung up.

Maria had sat quiet throughout the whole conversation, keeping the boys busy. Now I filled her in with everything Erika had told me. When I said I must pay her for the use of the phone, she looked at me as if I'd come from outer space.

Chapter 24

The candles on the kitchen window sill at Christmas burned extra bright. I placed the largest one I could find in the middle of the others and hoped Karl would spot it and it would shine and lighten the darkness wherever he and his fellow soldiers were this Christmas Eve. He had asked me to do this, in his letter, just in case he was not home by then and said he would be looking up at the sky and he would see it. I would do the same, just before it was time to light all the candles on the Christmas tree.

At last a letter had arrived. I noticed immediately that it had been opened and re-sealed before it was delivered to me. He said he was well and not to worry, asked me to be strong for him and the children and told me he would be home in a few weeks. He said he kissed my photograph every night and finished with, 'I love you, Fraulein Hilde.'

Egon had tried to work out where it was posted from but without success. We also hoped to get some clues by trying to read between the lines but did not learn anything at all. There was no date on it, so I did not know how long ago he wrote it, but imagined it was recent because of the mention of our Christmas tradition.

Maria had said: 'Families should be together at Christmas and we are your family, like it or not' she continued, 'but Egon and I are coming here and we are staying with you.' Before I could reply she added 'You have more space and three bedrooms, plus Egon will be working some of the time. You don't mind, do you?'

I hugged her and told her, 'Maria, I love it, why did I not think of that?'

'Because you never assume anything, but that is fine with me, I am supposed to be the one with all the bright ideas.'

'You are not still doing this crazy thing of yours, frankfurters and potato salad in the evening are you?' she asked with a slight concern showing on her face.

'Hopefully that will never change.' I replied. 'Wait until Egon tastes my potatoes, he will want to spend every Christmas Eve here after that.' I laughed when I said it but Maria didn't look that convinced.

As a surprise, two days before Christmas, Erika managed to take our mother with her to the office. She had asked for permission to phone me. Maria and Erika had arranged a time and it was up to Maria to make sure I was at her apartment when the call came in. Maria had pretended she needed some idea on what to get Egon and wanted to show me a couple of things.

My mother had never used a telephone before and sounded scared at first but then when she realised it was really me on the other end she started crying. For a while we both cried down the telephone lines using Erika's precious minutes until she finally intervened. 'Listen, Hilde, it took me a long time to convince mother I could arrange this, so please just speak, will you?'

Earlier in the day, I had carefully wrapped the presents for the children. Maria and I, we had decided to buy everything together and get them something nice. We got Klaus and Hugo soft toys, a lion for Klaus and a tiger for Hugo. Both made by Steiff. Renate got a doll which had a celluloid head and a soft body. Our hearts beat faster every time we walked into Frau Neuberger's toy shop, which they had repaired and restocked. She was always polite to us but we never received a gift from her again.

We had agreed not to buy presents for each other, but when I found a silver necklace for Inge with the rose symbols of our town, I just had to buy it. I also saw a striking two row multi-coloured Lucite - one which screamed 'Maria' at me when I took a closer look. I asked the shopkeeper to put it to one side and I collected it the next day.

Under the Christmas tree was also a parcel I received from Karl's parents.

Despite Maria's concern, Egon loved the dinner. The children played with their presents, Klaus going 'ROAR' and Hugo

'MEOW'. I was quietly thankful Karl's parents had thought about their grandchildren as all three children shared the chocolate which they had sent. For once I did not care if they were sick later.

We three drank some wine and listened to Christmas carols coming from the radio, occasionally joining in. I had put a very brave face on throughout the evening but could not stop crying when we sang Silent Night, praying that Karl would not be too lonely tonight of all nights.

Maria loved her necklace and at first looked cross, but then produced a small parcel from behind her and gave it to me with a 'Happy Christmas'. Inside the parcel was a delicate gold watch, with a round face and a gold bracelet.

'Maria,' I stared to say. She interrupted me and simply said, 'I did this for a selfish reason. The next time we arrange to meet somewhere you will have no excuse and you might actually be on time.'

'Hilde, look,' said Egon and pointed to the children. Renate had stood up all on her own. She turned, looked at me and walked holding her dolly. 'Mamma, baby,' she said and gave it to me. I put my arm around her and kissed her on the head. She would be one year old in a few days and she was already walking.

Chapter 25

'Karl, is this really you? Tell me I am not dreaming and when I open my eyes, you will still be there.' Karl had no chance to reply. Klaus opened the bedroom door, ran over to the bed, climbed on and got between us. 'Pappa come home,' he said.

'Yes, Pappa is home,' said Karl and pulled him close. I heard rattling from Renate's cot and got up. 'You might as well have the whole family in bed with you,' I said.

Karl had arrived late at night. I did not hear him knocking at the door and jumped when I saw a figure through the glass and a voice said, 'Let me in Fraulein Hilde.'

My scream woke the children who immediately started crying. 'This is what I call a welcoming committee.' He said, laughing when at last I was in his arms.

In the morning I asked Frau Bucker whether she could go and cancel Inge from coming over whilst I took the children and went to see Maria, hoping she would be in. I wrapped the children up warm and took them both by the hand and hoped Renate could manage it. The pushchair would be too difficult to manoeuvre through the snow, which was still on the ground and it was already the end of February.

Maria took one look at me, smiled and said, 'I guess Karl is at home.'

'How did you know that?' I asked.

'Well, who is supposed to be the clairvoyant here?' she reminded me of what I had said previously. 'Come on, tell me,' she urged.

'He got home last night.'

'And?'

'And what?' I teased her. I had not felt this happy for a long time.

'And did he tell you anything?' she asked.

'To be honest we have not talked much yet.' I said still smiling. 'He is sleeping right now. If Egon is not working tonight, why don't you come over for dinner?'

'Let's make it tomorrow. You two should be alone, just you and your children tonight.'

The next evening we ate the lentil stew I had prepared and Karl repeated most of what he had told me the previous afternoon.

'I am going to join the 7th Panzer Division in a few days,' he told us. 'I am awaiting new orders and will be stationed at my previous office here in town until then.'

'Why Karl?' It was Egon who asked. 'Why are you joining the 7th Panzer Division?' It took Karl quite a while before he said, 'I can't go back to Poland, I can't do it, Egon.'

'Who is commanding the 7th Panzer Division?' Egon continued questioning.

'General Erwin Rommel.'

'General Rommel?' I said, 'Do you know him?'

'Yes,' Karl said 'during the last few weeks I served under him. This is why I am joining that Division.'

'Where will this Division go?' Egon wanted to know.

'I really don't know and if I did I would not be able to tell you, so please don't ask me.' Egon gave him a suspicious look.

'Honestly, Egon, I don't know.'

'You are right, Karl, let's not think about it. But wherever you have got to go, please keep safe.'

'I don't even know how long I will be here,' Karl said.

Renate was due another check up and I was glad Karl could come with me this time. Egon greeted us and together we went to see the paediatrician I had met before on a couple of occasions. Renate's previous results looked encouraging and I hoped for the same news today.

'Dr Bernward, I would like you to meet my husband.' I beamed when I said it.

'Herr Paekel, it is good to meet you. Your wife has filled you in I presume?'

I think Karl was dumbfounded by the dismissive attitude the doctor displayed towards me. Karl ignored her totally and said 'Hilde, let Dr Bernward see for herself what Renate has achieved.'

I had to smile. I took Renate to the other end of the room, stood her on the floor and whispered into her ear 'Nate, go to Pappa.' I did not need to say that twice as off she toddled into her father's outstretched arms.

'Yes, as I was going to say, the treatment seems to be working. Do you mind if I just examine her?'

After the visit we had a coffee and a piece of cake in the doctor's canteen at the hospital.

'I know Dr Bernward is coming across rather abruptly' said Egon 'but please believe me when I say she is a very competent paediatrician who is an expert in the field of hormone imbalance.'

'Egon, you worry too much, I am really thankful and without your help, I do not know what I would have done.' I put my hand on his to emphasise what I said.

Of course I understood Karl had to go and see his parents but I was a little surprised when he suggested the children and I come along. I was not ready to face them again and I silently blamed them for not having made any effort to see the children or to find out how I was coping without Karl. Karl did not say as much but maybe he thought I also should have made contact with his parents. He would never know that his mother had wanted me to live over one thousand kilometres away on my own with their grandchild.

'Karl, why don't you take Klaus with you? He would love to spend the time with his father, not to mention to travel in a jeep. And I'm sure your parents would love to meet their grandson.' I knew the last statement hurt him, but I thought that was nothing compared to our children having been denied their grandparents up to now.

83

Chapter 26

Four weeks, four weeks of wedded bliss, that was exactly how long Karl stayed. One day he received new orders and the next day he was gone.

He went by train this time. I did not accompany him to the railway station.

He outright forbade me to go with him. At first I felt hurt but afterwards I understood. If I did not know which direction his train took, I could not possibly know which area he had to report to. We also decided not to tell Maria and Egon, until after he had left.

We had spent our weeks together as if in a trance. We pretended everything was as it should be and nothing was wrong at all. We had dinner with former colleagues of Karl's, went dancing at the dancehall, *Haus vier Linden* , which had become a very popular venue in recent months. A place to go and forget your worries, even if it was only for a few hours. Together with Maria and Egon we visited the theatre to see *Die Fledermaus* by Johann Strauss. Frau Bucker was always happy to look after the children during these evenings.

And then back to reality. Karl had gone again and realisation hit me. Germany was at War.

We now listened to the Radio as often as we could. We had found the BBC Overseas Service, which was broadcast in German. We usually waited until Inge had gone and the children were in bed. Maria, Frau Bucker and I would turn the sound down, fearing to be overheard. We even made sure the curtains were drawn and the lights were out.

Sometimes I found it hard to make sense of what we heard. During the day we got bombarded with reports from our official German channel, although it was clearly a propaganda exercise, it seemed to be very effective. At night we heard the same events but totally different facts.

On the 10th May 1940, I heard the following words spoken by Propaganda Minister Goebbels during the day:

'Citizens, our brave troops are fighting back at the borders with France. Leading this Battle is the 7th Panzer Brigade under the command of General Erwin Rommel, assisted by the 38 Infantry Division. The 26th, 19th and 32nd Divisions are defending the borders at the Low Countries together with the brave soldiers of our allies, Italy. There have been very few casualties reported so far. Our thoughts are with our Fuehrer and our brave troops. Heil Hitler!'

I was alone at my apartment when I heard the announcement, for which I was grateful. Now I knew where Karl was, in France with the 7th Panzer Brigade.

I could not have faced anybody at that moment. It was only Klaus and Renate who kept me sane that day. Inge, Frau Bucker, Maria, Egon, all knocked at the door, shouting to let them in. But I just sat there, not even preparing any food for the children.

In the evening when they still had not heard any movement from inside, Egon brought the locksmith over and they removed the lock, stormed their way into the sitting room and found me just sitting there.

'Egon, what are we going to do?' I asked him when he stood in front of me.

'I have no idea, but what I do know is, what we are not going to do, and that is fall apart. Now get up and take care of your children,' was his reply.

I looked around and saw surprise on everybody's face at his harsh words, but that was exactly what I needed.

'Let's make some dinner we can talk afterwards' said Maria, followed by 'I will do it.'

'Oh no, please don't!' shouted Egon, who was busy repairing the lock at the door.

'Let me take care of the children, Hilde, you cook. I have some minced meat upstairs, let me fetch it.' Frau Bucker was already out of the door on her way upstairs before she finished her sentence.

Later that evening we listened to the BBC's version of events and talked until midnight.

Chapter 27

I felt blessed having such good friends and I wanted to do something for them. I suggested we took a trip to Goslar. If we went by train it would take just over one and half hours. Suddenly I needed more than just climbing up the stairs of the tower in our woodland here and I looked longingly in the direction of where Goslar would be.

I had not been there for almost four years and the time was right for me to go back. I hoped it was just as I remembered. I could show my friends around and take them for coffee and cake to the *Hotel Achtermann* or, if the café was still open, near the Imperial Palace. Maybe I could introduce them to the café owner. Would they still have the music afternoons I so much enjoyed?

I wanted to pay for the train fare for Inge, but Maria and Frau Bucker insisted that the three of us paid for her fare together and we agreed on a date which was suitable for all of us. Maria suggested the 22nd May 1940, which was my 28th birthday.

We were lucky, the sun was shining and our spirits were high. We made some sandwiches and took a flask with cold tea and drinks for the children. Frau Bucker had a wicker picnic basket, which had metal cups and plates. It had enough space for some of the food and the napkins. We placed everything onto the back of Renate's pushchair and took the early train to make the most of our day out.

I could not keep still for one minute once we got there. I showed them the Imperial Palace and we walked around the market square. Klaus and Hugo went running along, enjoying the space and freedom. Renate was in her pushchair most of the time.

Goslar had not changed and they immediately understood why I fell in love with this town. It was nestled between the mountains, making you feel safe, protected. I took them to the house I had lived in and we stood outside, quietly, for a while. I had told Maria and Frau Bucker a lot about my time here. We looked at each other and I knew they also wondered where Frau Lehmann was now and what had happened to her. I hoped that she was safe.

We had our picnic at the small lake at the *Zwinger*, the tower at the old wall which used to surround the town.

In the late afternoon we went looking for 'my' café. It was just like the last time I had been there. The little bell over the door gave a reassuring 'ding'. I recognised the owner straight away. He came over to show us to a seat, looked at me with a puzzled expression, then his face lit up. 'Fraulein Hilde!' he half asked, half exclaimed. 'You are Fraulein Hilde, aren't you?' he then asked when I had not immediately responded.

'Well, it is Frau Paekel now,' I said, smiling.

'You and Karl are married now, how wonderful,' he said excitedly.

'Yes and here are our children, Klaus and Renate,' I replied and I then introduced him to my friends.

He asked several questions all at once. 'How is Karl?' 'Do you live in Goslar now?' 'Have you heard from Frau Lehmann?'

I replied with questions of my own. 'Do you still have the musicians in the afternoon?' 'Do people still come and dance?'

'We have the afternoon dances every weekend, and the band still plays the same music, although the musicians are people you would not know. Some of the previous ones have gone on to bigger and better venues and some of them have just gone,' he added solemnly.

'Anyway, let me bring you some coffee and some fresh apple cake, then I will come and sit with you and we can talk. What would the children like?' he asked.

'Herr Schmitt, do you have any ice cream? They would love it,' said Maria.

We occupied the round table in the corner, with Klaus and Hugo at a little table right in front of us. They felt very grown up sitting on their own. Herr Schmitt left instructions not to be disturbed and I told him about the last four years. Like a waterfall it all came rushing out of me. Maria, Frau Bucker and Inge looked totally bewildered but did not interrupt.

Eventually Maria said, 'It's lucky that it's your birthday today, otherwise we would have stopped you quite a while back.'

'It is your birthday, Fraulein Hilde, sorry Frau Paekel. Let's celebrate. I will bring some drinks.' Herr Schmitt exclaimed and got up.

'Fraulein Hilde is just fine, I will always be Fraulein Hilde here, but I don't think I should have a drink right now.'

'Nor should I,' added Maria

'You're not, are you?' I looked at her when I asked the question.

'Are you?' she asked me instead.

'What? You're what?' asked Inge.

Frau Bucker rolled her eyes and said 'Inge, those two sitting there with a stupid grin on their faces, are pregnant.'

'A double reason to celebrate. Frau Bucker would you join me in a glass of the finest wine of the house? Inge, how old is Fraulein Inge? I am sure you could do with a little drink after that news. And two glasses of cold milk for the lucky ladies!'

Chapter 28

'Today, the 17th June 1940, France surrendered to our brave troops. Our Fuehrer has made a triumphant entrance into Paris. The streets were lined with people celebrating our victory. Today's success followed the hasty retreat of the British and their Allies from the beaches of Dunkirk. We have reports of heavy casualties to the enemy forces. Our thoughts are with our Fuehrer and our brave troops. Heil Hitler!'

Oh, Karl, where are you? Karl did not yet know we were having another child. I prayed that he would be able to hold it in his arms one day.

I spotted Maria from the kitchen window and waved to her. She looked very upset and I assumed she had heard the broadcast. I knew how worried she was about her brother in Brussels. He had joined the Belgian Resistance. I let her in and she immediately walked into the kitchen and sat at the table. Renate took Hugo by his hand. I gave the three children a biscuit each and they went off to play in the sitting room.

'Shall I stay a little longer?' shouted Inge from the hall. 'I could take the children and play outside.'

Maria indicated 'no'. 'It's alright, Inge, don't worry, I will see you tomorrow,' I said, going into the hall to see her off, making sure I left the sitting room door open so that we could watch the children from the kitchen.

'Goodbye, Inge,' shouted Maria.

'Goodbye,' said Inge.

'Pregnant or not', Maria then said 'I need a drink'.

'Maria, you'd better not.' I started to say then stopped when I saw how distressed she looked.

'What have you got to drink, Hilde?'

'I have a bottle of *Tokaj* wine I could open,' I replied.

'Oh yes and get two large glasses.'

I found the bottle and the corkscrew and got the glasses. Maria took the bottle from me and poured the wine. I got some bread, butter and cheese. I did not want the wine to go straight to our heads. Two drunken pregnant women in charge of three small children wouldn't do!

Normally I would ask what the matter was, but this time I waited until Maria was ready to talk.

She took a couple of sips. I could see tears filling her eyes. Eventually she said. 'Egon got his draft today. He has to report on Wednesday.'

'What! In two days? But he is a doctor.'

'You have heard about casualties, haven't you, Hilde?'

'Did they draft anybody else from the hospital,' I asked.

'Yes, two other surgeons' Maria replied.

'What about nurses?' I asked.

'There is a military medical division with their own trained nurses. It is based in Hamburg. That is where Egon will have to report to. From there on, we don't know.' she concluded.

'I am so sorry, Maria.' I just could not think of anything else to say. I knew exactly what she was feeling and what was foremost in her mind.

'Hilde, how do you cope?' she then asked me.

'I don't know, I really don't know. I assume I live day by day. The worst is, not knowing, not knowing where he is, not knowing whether he is alright, not knowing when he will be back.'

'Yes, that's what it will be like.' She had a really sad look in her eyes when she said it.

'Maria, the point is, I cope. I am surrounded by the best friends anybody could wish for. I do not feel alone, with everything that has happened so far, my friends are here for me. That is what it is like, Maria. We are there for each other.'

'With everything that has happened so far! What do you mean? Do you think it is going to continue?'

I could see she was so afraid.

'Maria, do you really believe Hitler will stop now?'

90

'No, of course not, but I hoped you would believe it and it might make me feel better.'

'I don't know how to put this' I continued 'but Egon will not be right at the front line. From the little I have learned, medical corps will usually be at the back.'

'Oh, Hilde, I am so sorry to burden you with all of this, I have totally forgotten to say, Egon would like you to bring Renate to the hospital tomorrow. He wants to arrange some tests before he goes and would like to introduce you to the doctor who will be looking after you besides the paediatrician.'

'Will you come with us?' I asked.

'Of course, don't forget we get a lot of feedback via the hospital and I must make sure we don't lose those contacts.' Maria raised her glass. 'Let's drink to Life!' she said.

Chapter 29

As if things weren't bad enough. It was already the beginning of July, no word from Karl and his mother and sister arrived unannounced for Klaus's third birthday.

Klaus ran towards them and put his little arms around his grandmother's legs. 'Oma!' he shouted happily. He must have made a really good impression when he met them a few months ago because she managed to raise a brief smile and patted him on the head.

'And this must be Renate,' Karl's sister Gertrud added stiffly, which prompted Renate to hide behind me.

They were still standing in the doorway as I slowly recovered from the shock of seeing them and stepped back so that they could enter.

'Has something happened to Karl?' I asked. I could not think of any other reason why they would have just turned up.

'I hope not and surely you would have informed us,' said his sour-faced sister.

'I came to see my grandson on his birthday' added Karl's mother finally.

Remembering the reception I received the only time I had met them, I said, 'What took you so long?'

I picked my frightened little girl up, held her tight and said 'Nate, say hello to your Oma and your Aunt Gertrud.' Instead of saying hello, she buried her face in my cardigan.

'I see you are pregnant again. You should not pick up a heavy child like that in your condition,' Gertrud almost spat at me. I could not even look at Karl's mother to see the reaction on her face.

I hadn't noticed the suitcase before, which was still standing behind them outside the apartment door. Oh no, I thought, surely they are not staying?

I nodded towards the case, looked at Gertrud and said sarcastically, 'I can see you are now guests in my house and I need to teach my children good manners.'

'That heavy child, as you put it, has a name 'Renate' and as you can see she is rather small. As for your suitcase, I can't help you with that,' I paused 'in my condition.'

Karl's mother came to her senses and said 'I am sorry, yes, we should have come before, but we are here now. Would it be alright if we stayed for two nights? We really would love to spend some time with the children. And you of course,' she added as an afterthought.

'Inge, would you please make some coffee for Karl's mother and sister? And would you mind going to the grocery store, at the corner? I will give you a list of what we need.

'Go via Maria,' I added quickly 'and remind her she is coming over this afternoon.'

Inge came from the kitchen, greeted the two still standing in the hall and went over to get the suitcase.

'No, it's alright, you don't need to do that. If you just make the coffee' I said to Inge.

'Please come in, I will show you where you can sleep tonight and you can freshen up,' I said to Karl's mother, ignoring Gertrud.

Karl's sister Gertrud took an instant dislike to the bubbling, full of life, Maria. Only when I stressed that Maria's husband was an important doctor, did she show a little interest.

Alone in the kitchen, Maria asked me, 'Is Gertrud married?' My face said it all.

'I'd better not stay for dinner,' she continued. 'This is your chance to get to know them.'

'To be honest, Maria, I already know them and you are not going to leave me in my hour of need.'

'In your hour of need?' Maria laughed. 'Alright, I'll stay.'

To their credit, they played with the children, and Klaus and Renate revelled at the attention they received. Karl's mother even made sure that Hugo did not feel left out.

Although it was a tense afternoon, the dinner went surprisingly well. I cooked a traditional Prussian dish of steamed hake with a mustard sauce, boiled potatoes and green beans, almost hoping they would not like it. To my amazement they ate everything, but not before they exchanged a puzzled look.

Just before the children's bedtime came a tentative knock on the door followed by, 'Let me in Fraulein Hilde.'

Klaus jumped up and before I could stop him he ran and opened the front door and was in his father's arms. 'Pappa come home,' he cried.

'Happy birthday, my son,' said Karl.

Chapter 30

I did not get to the hospital in time. Karl-Heinz was born on a very cold November night in 1940. I almost didn't even get back to my apartment. The air raid warning sirens had gone off. I was alone with the children and there was no chance I could make it to the designated areas. Frau Bucker came racing downstairs, banging her fists on the door. I nearly missed her but she heard Renate cry and knew I was at home.

When I let her in she rushed over, grabbed a blanket, wrapped it around Renate and picked her up whilst I calmly got Klaus dressed.

'Hilde, what are you doing? There is no time. Get a bedcover and pillows, let's go.' she urged.

I buckled over in pain, my contractions had started.

'Oh no! Not now!' she said when she saw me. 'We can't risk getting as far as to the air raid shelter. Let's go into the cellar.' With that she took charge and marched me downstairs.

Several of our neighbours were already there and moved over to make some space for us to put our pillows down to sit on and cover the children with the blanket and duvet.

'Did you see any planes coming over?' asked one neighbour. 'Was there anything on the radio warning us about an imminent attack?' asked another.

Before I even sat down my waters broke and I cried out. All I could focus on was Klaus's frightened face.

'Mamma!' he cried out, lifting his arms up to me.

'It's alright, Klaus. Mamma is not ill, but you are having a new baby brother or sister.' I tried to sound convincing, although I did not feel very confident myself. I did not want to give birth to my baby in a damp dark cellar in the middle of an air raid.

Frau Bucker gave out a loud sigh and said to the neighbour sitting next to her, 'Can we leave Renate and Klaus with you? Air raid or not we had better get back upstairs.'

Klaus was not going to be left behind and I almost gave in and took the children with me but another neighbour stepped in. 'Hilde, he will be better off here. It's dark but it's safer. Come, Klaus, you sit with me.' When that didn't get any reaction she said, 'I will tell you a story and let's light some candles.' That settled it.

Young Hannelore from the top floor, where she lived with her grandparents, stood up and said, 'I will come with you, you might need extra help.'

Everybody looked at her, she shrugged her shoulders and continued 'I can boil water and I can fetch towels.'

Her grandmother looked at her in amazement. But Hannelore was not to be put off. 'That's what you do, is that not right?'

'Yes, Hannelore, that's right. I am glad you are coming with us' Frau Bucker said with an encouraging smile.

The air raid was a false alarm but my contractions were real.

'Hannelore, could you find some music on the radio, it might take Hilde's mind off the next contractions' she said and when she saw my look she continued, 'Or it might not, but it will help me.'

'What is your favourite name?' I asked her when she held my hand.

'I had a little boy once. His name was Karl-Heinz.' The sad look on her face almost tore me apart. I felt ashamed, we had been close for so long and I knew nothing about her.

If it is a boy, Karl-Heinz it is,' I said. 'Please can you take one of my front door keys, I don't know what I would do without you.' We both held each other crying openly.

In the evening I held my little boy in my arms and listened to Lale Anderson singing 'Lili Marlene.' My heart ached, I so much wanted Karl to be here. I didn't even know whether he liked the name Karl-Heinz.

Chapter 31

There was no need to worry. Karl did like the name Karl-Heinz. I had no idea how he got my letter. When Karl was not at home I wrote in my diary and read it to him when he was here. I did not want him to miss all the little things our children learned every day. I wanted to make sure he was part of our daily family life. Sometimes I let Klaus and Renate do a few scribbles under an entry or I enclosed a little drawing Klaus had made, he seemed to have a particular talent with coloured crayons.

After Karl-Heinz was born I copied what I had written in my book and sent Karl a letter. Klaus was only three and half years old but he insisted I taught him to write, 'Pappa come home' at the bottom of it, and Renate wanted to add her name as well.

I wrote his name and rank on the letter and put it into a larger envelope and posted it to General Rommel's Headquarters in Munich. It found Karl and I got a reply. This time his letter had not been opened prior to delivery. No blacked out words.

I read it several times a day. It made me feel like I could touch him by just holding the letter. I imagined his smell when I put the letter against my face. Karl was coming home. He applied for leave and it was granted. He would be here either for Christmas or just after.

I was so excited when I told Maria, almost forgetting that she had not heard one word from Egon since he left six months ago. Every time I took Renate to see the doctor in charge of her case at the hospital, Maria came with me. Whilst I was waiting to be seen, Maria would seek out everybody she knew, hoping somebody had some news from their colleagues who went with Egon at that time.

Maria gave birth to Manfred, two weeks after Karl-Heinz was born, all alone at the hospital.

She had phoned one of the nurses during the day and they sent a car to pick her up. A girl from the hospital reception looked after Hugo. I was heartbroken that I was not near my friend when she needed me.

Maria tried to console me by saying, 'Hilde, you just had a baby yourself.'

'Maria, stop being so reasonable all the time. I could have had Hugo, that's what I could have done. You had better not do this again. Next time, send somebody to get me.'

'I'm not going to have another one,' she said.

'I mean "anything" Maria, and now let me hold little Manfred for a while.'

The garrison Karl was to report to whilst he was at home, was at the corner of our street. And it actually did have a lamp post outside, just like in the song, 'Lili Marlene'. We had dinner one evening at the Officers Mess during his home leave and walked home through the snow. We both looked at the lamp post at the same time and ran towards it but he let me reach it first. I leaned against it, looking at him and sang, '*Underneath the lantern......*'

When I finished all verses, I saw how affected he was by it, tears streaming down his face and he said, 'Hilde, what if...'

'Don't say it Karl, don't you ever say it.'

During the last day of his leave, we took Klaus and Renate to 'our' tower accompanied by Maria and Hugo. Inge was happy to look after the two babies, especially since Hannelore from upstairs was always willing to help. Hannelore came nearly every day to check on Karl-Heinz. Karl and I had decided to ask her to become his godmother.

We felt the crisp cold air on our faces and the snow crunching under our feet. Karl pulled the sledge with Renate on it, while the boys were running in and out of snowdrifts and making snowballs, throwing them towards the adults. Only when a couple of them hit Renate did we have to put a stop to it.

We were surprised how busy it was around the tower. Mothers with their children, sliding down the hill on their sledges, pulling them back up. Again and again. Karl took both of the boys and joined the rest. A few times the boys had to wait when it was Renate's turn.

But it was just Karl and me who climbed to the top of the tower, taking in the view from above and pointing towards Goslar.

That is where he told me he was going to be posted to Africa to join the Panzer Brigade in Tunis. 'General Erwin Rommel has been promoted to Field Marshal. He is going to form the Africa Corps. I've just been informed,' he added. He realised what a shock it was for me and how upset I was with this news.

'But, Africa, Karl! When can you possibly come home to see your children, when you are so far away in Africa?'

He held me tight. 'Please be brave, Hilde. I will come home. I promise.'

Chapter 32

Erika told me on the phone that she had a letter for me from Oleg. I suggested she open it and send it to me in a new envelope and post it without a return address or any other notes from her. She seemed puzzled by my request but said she would do it.

'Don't read it,' I told her.

'Hilde, why do you think I would want to read your letters? I am not interested in what Oleg says to you.' I could hear how hurt she was by what I had just said.

'You know that is not it. We don't know what is in that letter, and if you are ever questioned about it, you really wouldn't know,' I explained.

'Hilde, who would question me about what Oleg says to you?' As always, Erika was not going to be fobbed off. She always was inquisitive, which was one of the things I loved about her.

'Erika, for somebody as bright as you, you can be very slow sometimes. I assume this letter comes from Poland? And Germany is at War?'

'Oh, now I understand. Of course I will do it, just as you said.'

'I am going to write to Oleg. Maybe he should not post his letters for you to pass on, it's too risky,' I said.

'Hilde, I am eighteen years old, you no longer have to look after me, really,' she laughed.

'That reminds me, how is this boyfriend of yours?' I then asked.

'He is just a friend, not my boyfriend. I told you that before.' She sounded a little cross now, I thought, maybe there was more to it than she let on.

'Has he got a name, this 'friend' of yours?' I now teased her.

'Yes, he has, his name is Erich.'

A lot of what Oleg said in his letter I had to guess through implication, but from what I could make out he had not heard from

Harel and his family for some time, but since he was going to make a delivery nearby in a few weeks he would make a point of finding out. I knew Harel, Karina and their children lived in the centre of Warsaw, although Oleg did not say so in his letter.

Oleg's biggest worry was that Ludmilla, his wife, was now required to wear the Star of David on her clothing with 'Jude' on it. She had one on her coat and now did not want to leave the house. She would not even take the children to school. They made arrangements with her neighbour that Ludmilla would do the cleaning and washing and the neighbour would take the children to and from school and do the shopping. Since the children were only half-Jewish this seemed to be alright, for now, he said. Sometimes Ludmilla seemed to get depressed, he observed, although she would not admit it. She would no longer visit the grave of Oleg's mother, something she did every week together with the children. Oleg tried his best to find the time to take them, but then felt heart-broken leaving Ludmilla behind.

Having seen what was happening in Poland to most of the Jewish stores, Ludmilla's father gave his business to Oleg, They changed the name and the sign over the stores. One of Oleg's brothers and his cousins had joined the Polish Army.

He finished his letter with,'Hilde, I am really worried about my family, pray for us.'

I did pray for them and I prayed that Erika had listened to me and had not read this letter.

Chapter 33

We did not want to hear the daily radio broadcast, but we felt we had to. This was the only way to find out a little bit of what was going on. The three of us: Maria, Frau Bucker and I, tried to make sure we had the chance to listen together. Sometimes Inge was there as well, but on those occasions we only listened to the broadcast from the German Armed Forces. We were careful what we said when Inge was around. She was still in her late teens and we did not want to influence or compromise her. Inge's official time with me had passed some months ago, and I was sent a new girl from the female section of the Hitler Youth. I was terrified. Being the wife of an Officer I had no choice in the matter and had to accept the help.

But Inge insisted she would stay, although she was now an apprentice book keeper at the office of the local Sugar Refinery. We were so grateful about her decision to come and spend her free time with me and the children that we decided to treat her to a lunch at the little restaurant not far from 'my tower.'

Exactly one week after my 29th birthday was the day we had picked for our outing. We were quite a sight, walking up the narrow roads through the woods. Hugo and Klaus running ahead as usual, Renate toddling after them trying to catch up; two prams, one being pushed by Inge and one by Hannelore, who was not going to be left behind especially since her God-son Karl-Heinz would most definitely need her, she said. We three women at the back of the group, laughing and joking.

It was already busy when we got there. Mothers with children, some grandmothers who were rocking prams to keep the younger ones quiet. A couple of elderly men. Maria knew the owner and went over to speak to him. He pointed inside but Maria shook her head, pointing to a group of tables at the corner on the veranda which looked like the people were just leaving. The owner nodded and indicated five minutes with his hand.

From our table we could see the top of the tower. As soon as we sat down I kept staring at it. Maria noticed it, laughed and said 'Inge, just change places with Hilde, will you. This tower is like a magnet to her. We will not hear one word from Hilde, if she keeps looking in that direction. Goslar is behind you, if you need to know,' she continued, now looking at me.

Hannelore took Karl-Heinz from his pram and placed him on her knees, but he kept wriggling, wanting to stand up. He had been crawling for the last week and loved being able to move around.

'Can I take him to play on the grass over there?' she asked.

'Yes, of course, but don't go too far. The food will be here soon,' I said.

'Can we go?' asked Klaus, looking at Hugo.

'Yes but stay with Hannelore,' we agreed.

'Me come' said Renate.

'No, little one' Frau Bucker had Renate on her lap. 'You stay here. You feel a little bit hot.'

'Does she?' I touched her forehead, she did feel hot and her nose started to run. 'I will take her to see the doctor if she is not better by tomorrow.'

The food arrived and we looked over to where Hannelore was standing with the children and saw her arguing with a group of young men. I stood up to get her but she had already gathered the children and came over to where we sat, followed by a rowdy group of Hitler Youth.

'What was that all about?' I asked her.

'Nothing.'

The leader of the group stayed behind her and walked over to our table. 'Fraulein,' he said to Hannelore. 'You have a fine blond German boy there, pure blood, from what I can see, you make sure he stays that way and does not mix with any Jews. Otherwise we will get him.' He said proudly, pointing at his companions all wearing the uniform and swastikas.

I started to get up but was beaten to it by an elderly gentleman. 'You lot run along and leave these good people alone. You should be ashamed of yourselves.'

It was like the youth had waited for a confrontation like that. He walked over to the older man, grabbed him by the jacket, pulled him forward and proclaimed, 'You better watch it, Jew. You have to wear the yellow star soon, showing everybody what you are. Watch out at night, Be glad only your windows got damaged last time.'

With horror I now recognised Frau Nuernberger from the toy shop and her father. This time I had to stand up for them. Maria gave me a worried look but accompanied me when I walked over. All the other people around us saw what was going on but nobody moved.

I touched the youth on his shoulder and he spun round. Before his fist could hit my face Herr Nuernberger had tackled him to the ground. Now the other customers were jumping up, knocking their chairs over. The nearest table to us fell against the wall spilling the half-eaten lunches onto the floor. By now the owner rushed over and helped Herr Nuernberger back on his feet and then marched the youth to the open gate.

'Fritz! Come on, let's go,' said one of them.

But Fritz was not about to lose face. He tried to get back in and spat in my direction with, 'I am going to report you, Jew lover!'

Although I was shaking inside, I calmly walked towards him and replied, 'Much better Fritz, it is Fritz, right ? I am going to see your Hitler Youth leader tomorrow morning. Let's see what he thinks about the behaviour of one of his charges.' That had the right effect. Like the cowards they were, they all started running away.

Frau Nuernberger was by now standing next to me, took my hand and said, 'Thank you. I will never forget what you just did for us.'

Chapter 34

We were silent most of the way home. Everybody wrapped in their own thoughts. I felt sorry that Hannelore had to witness the confrontation at the restaurant and I said so at some stage.

But Hannelore , being really brave, replied, 'I am glad I did, that only confirmed what I thought about them in the first case and it is best to know, isn't it?' she then asked.

We agreed but told her it was wiser to keep her opinion just between us, there was no need to worry her grandparents. They might not understand. Hannelore beamed with pride.

I was getting worried about Renate, she refused to walk, felt very hot and her neck started to swell up. Her skin seemed to have a bluish tint. By the time we got to the bottom of our road, she had difficulty breathing.

I picked her up, and told the others I would take her to the Military Infirmary at the Garrison where Karl had been based. I ran to the gate and the soldier on guard was the son of the owner from the corner shop where he had served us many times before he joined the army. He recognised me immediately and opened the gate. He then told one of the other guards to take over, whilst he took the jeep and drove us the rest of the way.

'I'd better come in with you, otherwise they might not let you in. There has been extra tight security imposed today.'

'Why?' I managed to ask, trying to keep up with him.

He stopped briefly turned his head and asked, 'You don't know?'

'Know what?' But before he could reply, the doors swung open towards us and we were inside. The amount of people around and the noise was overwhelming. Renate started to cry. We had to fight our way through and found a nurse.

He looked at her name attached to her uniform and said, 'Nurse Weiner, I have a very sick child here.'

She looked at me and said 'Sorry we can't take any civilians today, try the main hospital in town.'

I was just going to turn around when I heard him say, 'Frau Paekel's husband is an Officer who is based here when he is on home leave.'

She went bright red. 'I am sorry, please bring her over here, what is the matter with her?'

'She has a fever, her throat seems to be infected. It is swollen and to me her skin looks slightly blue. Oh, yes, and she has difficulties breathing.'

She finally took a look, found an empty trolley, turned towards the young soldier and said, 'Thank you, I will take it from here.' With that he was dismissed.

'Thank you for your all your help,' I quickly added before he disappeared.

'Nurse Weiner' I asked 'Do you know what is wrong with my daughter?'

'I think she has diphtheria. It is highly contagious. You have to come with me.' I stood frozen, holding on to Renate and I did not move.

'Frau Paekel, we have to get her into isolation, there is no time to lose. Please come with me.' She hurried on. I had to follow otherwise I would have lost sight of her in the crowd. We went through some corridors and several sets of doors until we reached the isolation ward. There the doctors took over.

'We have to run some tests and then make your daughter comfortable, you can see her soon. Meanwhile there are some forms which need to be filled out and then we have to test you as well.' At least I think that is what they told me. It seemed like it was not me who this was happening to but instead I was watching somebody else from a distance. 'Can you give us your daughter's name, birth date and her medical history,' somebody else asked. All the while I heard my little girl whimpering and calling me.

'Frau Paekel, Frau Paekel!' This time I heard them and started to give all the information they needed.

Somebody took me gently by the arm, 'Renate will be fine. You brought her to the right place. We have already many cases here. You can see her every day.'

'I can see her every day?' I asked. 'Surely I can take her home tonight?'

'If Renate has diphtheria she has to stay in isolation for about six weeks. There could be added complications. We have to test her to find out whether she is also a carrier of the disease and if she is we have to treat that too. Meanwhile you also need to be tested and everybody you came in close contact with. Do you have any other children?' The questions just kept coming.

On the way to the laboratory for my test I heard a soldier shouting across the room. 'Sir, the death toll is over 2000 and some have been taken prisoners.'

An ice-cold feeling went right through me. 'Sorry, what did the soldier just say?' I asked.

'The British sank the Bismarck today in the North Atlantic. Most on board have perished. The few survivors were taken as Prisoners of War.'

A nurse accompanied me home, late at night. Everybody was still there, by now very worried because it had been several hours since I had taken Renate to the Garrison. We needed to wake the children so that the nurse could take the test, some swabs from their nasal passages. We were instructed not to leave the apartment until the results were known. The test should only take one day.

The nurse promised to send somebody to Inge's mother and to inform her place of work .We knew it would be dramatic for Inge's mother to be woken in the middle of the night, she immediately would fear the worst. Inge's father had been drafted just over one month ago.

We sat up all night, drinking coffee, and going over the events of the day again and again. We listened to both of the radio broadcasts that night, something we had never done with Inge and Hannelore around. They did not even know that Maria was fluent in English.

Chapter 35

All I could do during the next six weeks was watch helplessly through a glass window at the isolation ward. The first two weeks were critical and most of the time Renate did not know where she was, or whether I was there. Then she became stronger and wanted her mother. She would spot me arriving and the nurse helped her to climb onto a chair so she could put her little hands where I had placed mine on the other side of the glass. If I spoke loud enough, she could hear me. She was only two and a half years old but she soon realised her Mamma was not here to take her home. From experience she knew when you fell and had a hurt, Mamma would make it better by blowing on it three times, showing an extra finger after every blow. Then Mamma would say, 'See, there it is flying away. Gone.' Sometimes you even got a sticking plaster. Mamma called it a 'trophy' but where was her Mamma now?

She solved the problem by ignoring me. When she spotted me a quick smile would cross her face, but then she remembered, went to her bed and sat on it with her back towards me. When she was really distressed she would cover her ears with her hands when I spoke to her.

That did it for me. Isolation or not, I opened the door and stormed inside, picked up my little girl and held her close. 'Mamma is here,' I said over and over again. At first she resisted but Renate was very forgiving and soon rewarded me by holding onto me very tightly.

The nurse went and got a doctor, who was still in his operating gown with his facemask on.

'Get out!' he shouted. 'You can't come in here risking infecting yourself and others.'

I must have sounded like the old hysterical fishwife, back home in East Prussia when I screamed 'You said six weeks, and it has been almost six weeks now!' Then added, calmer, 'I must thank you for what you did, but I am taking her with me today.'

The next day I started to plan a little celebration for the following evening. This was my way to show my friends how much I appreciated all the extra help during the last few weeks. Maria, as always, was offering to assist me, but this time I insisted she was just my guest the same as everybody else. She did, however, insist we go into town together to get everything I needed and maybe we should go and get a game so that the older children could play together.

We went to the toy shop first, since this was the furthest one away and it struck us how dark it looked from some distance.

'They don't usually close on a Thursday,' said Maria.

'There is a notice on the door. Maybe there is a religious holiday today, or they have gone visiting some relatives,' was all I could think of.

The shop was in total darkness, there were no colourful toys displayed in the window. From what we could see all the toys had been packed into boxes and stored at the back. The yellow notice attached to the inside of the door simply said 'CLOSED'.

Maria was uncharacteristically quiet that evening. When everybody had gone she said 'Hilde, can we stay tonight?'

When I didn't reply immediately she quickly added, 'The children are already asleep and it would be a shame to wake them.'

'I am surprised that after all this time, you still think you need to ask me that. You know I want you to stay, but I am afraid that you think I take your life over completely,' I replied.

'I got a letter today.' Maria said.

'What sort of letter?'

'I don't know.'

'What do you mean, you don't know?'

'I haven't opened it.'

'You haven't opened it? Who is it from?' I asked.

'It is from the War Ministry, it is in my bag. I will get it.' she said.

Her hands were shaking when she handed it to me. It was a large brown envelope, with an official seal, and it felt that there was something else inside.

'You have to open it, Maria.' I handed it to her.

'Hilde, can you do it for me? I can't, otherwise I will take it home as it is and look at it every day, wondering.'

I closed my eyes for a brief moment trying to gather some strength and took the letter.

Inside was what looked like another letter. I took it out and looked at it. I recognised Egon's handwriting.

'Maria,' I whispered 'it is a letter from Egon,' but she did not register what I said.

'Maria, it is a letter from Egon,' I repeated.

'A letter from Egon? Are there any other notes with it?'

I turned the large envelope upside down and shook it. 'No.'

Maria finally took the letter.

'There is some wine left in the kitchen,' I said. 'I'll pour us a glass each. Meanwhile, please read your letter' and with that I got up and left Maria sitting alone with her thoughts.

She was crying when I got back. I put the drinks down, rushed over and started to comfort her. 'I am so sorry,' I said.

Maria looked up at me, smiling. 'No, it is not that. Egon is in England he has been taken as a Prisoner of War.'

'What?'

'Yes, he is a Prisoner of War, somewhere in South England, here read it for yourself.' She wiped her face and nose with her sleeve and handed me the letter.

The majority of what he wrote had been blacked out, but yes he had been taken to England. How and when had been deleted with censorship markings. He was treated well and he had got the job of looking after the other prisoners' welfare. She was not to worry, he would write again. He wanted to know what their new baby was and what he or she was called. He finished the letter by telling her how much he loved her and to kiss the children from their father.

Maria was ecstatic, the first time in over one year she was laughing and singing, we were so noisy we had neighbours knocking on the door asking whether we were alright.

That night she wanted to start a diary, just like mine.

After some time we calmed down and I said, 'I didn't know England had taken any prisoners. When did that start?' Then it dawned on me, 'The Bismarck' I said. 'There were survivors when the Bismarck was sunk about two months ago and Egon did have to report to Hamburg, right?'

Chapter 36

I waited for another letter from Oleg to arrive. Erika said she posted it. She told me life in our hometown had become even more difficult since Hitler had broken his agreement with Stalin and attacked Russia. This was of course not the way it was portrayed in the newsreels in the cinemas, or on the German Forces channels. We still listened to two different broadcasts and then drew our own conclusions. Tilsit, she said, was swarming with soldiers. It had been turned into the main Infantry base in the North. Food was getting scarce for most people and our smallholding had been broken into twice. They had stolen live animals and large amounts of vegetables. She complained to the local Town Hall, where she worked and since then, every so often, a military patrol drove past and checked with them, making sure everything was in order. Now she was sorry she said something. Our father went mad, she said, when he found out that it was her fault that the military come snooping around.

'Her' Erich was now also in the army, he had no choice in the matter. She did not know where he was, but was afraid it would be Russia. She definitely wanted to stay in Tilsit now, otherwise how would he find her when he came home?

Oleg could not find any sign of Harel and his family on his first visit. He went to their address and rang the apartment's bell on the door, but there was no reply. When he drove away, he could see movement behind a curtain in the apartment below Harel's. He went there again later in the day and this time tried the neighbour as well. Realising Oleg would not give up, an old man finally opened the window and said: 'Go away, they have gone, we don't know anything.' He slammed the window closed and drew the curtains, to make the point that Oleg would not get any information out of him.

Some weeks later, Oleg returned and tried again to speak to their neighbour. This time the old man looked and just walked away ignoring Oleg's pleas. Across the road two elderly women left their building and came over.

'We have seen you here before, you are Polish?' When they were sure he was, they told him.

'Soldiers came late at night in two lorries which were full of people, all sitting quietly, huddled together. The vehicles stopped outside. Uniformed men with rifles stormed the building, knocking on doors waking everybody up and checking each apartment. Harel, Karina and their children were the only ones escorted out, each carrying a small case. They were then pushed forward and forced to join the others. Nobody has seen them since.'

This is how Oleg related it to me in his letter.

Chapter 37

'Did you hear that?' Maria and I were in my kitchen baking. That is, I was baking and Maria was watching but only after she had fed the children. Five little mouths to feed and ten sticky hands was not an easy task. Klaus and Hugo considered themselves 'big' boys and did not want any help.

'We can do it.' they insisted as they got their chairs, placed them in front of the dining table, sat down and waited patiently. Considering that the milk only spilled over once and the mashed potatoes stayed mainly on their spoons, they considered it a job well done. They took their dirty plates to the sink, pushed the chairs back and announced 'We are going into the living room, we have to play now!'

We tried very hard not to laugh.

Renate of course had to keep up with the boys. 'I do it,' she said and walked over to get her chair, which was too heavy and would almost have fallen over if I had not reached it in time. She was happy when I told her she could help me make a cake.

We were baking for Inge's younger brother's school Fete. Every year the school would hold it in the Autumn. All the children would meet at the Town Square. The girls would wear a dirndl and have their hair braided with flowers. Most boys would wear their lederhosen. The school band would be playing and two by two, led by their teachers, the procession would march toward the tower. When they got there, games would be played whilst the adults laid out the food on the first level of the tower base. This was just the right height. The best thing was the walk back into town in the dark with every child carrying a handmade, candle-lit lantern.

'You do realise the tower door will be locked that day,' Maria reminded me when I quickly agreed to come along the day Inge asked us. I even volunteered to bake some cakes.

114

'Maria, I will do anything to be near the tower, you should know that by now,' I laughed in reply.

'Anyway, did I hear what?' I now asked her. I was still engrossed with my cake mix and trying to stop Renate sticking her fingers into the bowl and licking it. That was her idea of helping.

'On Radio Belgrade, they said something about Field Marshal Rommel.'

'Did they?' I turned round, as if that would help me to hear what had been said.

'Leave it on, maybe they will say it again. In any case we like to listen to Lili Marlene.' The song had finished and we both kept quiet and waited.

' *This is an announcement for all our troops listening to us, especially the ones serving in North Africa and to their families back home. Make sure you tune into Radio Belgrade in the evening. We will be ending our program every night at 21.57 hours precisely, with Lale Anderson singing for you, 'Lili Marlene'. We are happy to comply with Field Marshal Rommel's wishes. '*

The Town Square was full of excited children running around. Mothers and grandparents were trying to put them into some sort of order and fussing about them. Teachers were shouting and issuing instructions. The band was assembling and practising. Not to mention all the onlookers, family and friends. The younger ones, ours included, were playing hide-and-seek in amongst the school children. The boys from the Hitler Youth were loading wooden carts with bags containing balls, small goal posts, and bags holding all sorts for the games which had been planned. Plus, the prepared food and bottles of milk and cocoa.

The sound of music, mixed with laughter, was infectious. Soon we had to take our children by the hand and follow the procession. Our little gathering was a large enough group on its own.

Five lively children and five adults. Hannelore was included in the adult count. It should have taken just over one hour to reach our destination. The whole procession came to a sudden stop, long before we reached the grassy area which was going to be used.

After a while Hannelore offered to have a look what the holdup was and ran ahead. The children wanted to go as well, of course, but we persuaded them to wait a little longer. Hannelore would be back soon.

'We can't go there today,' she told us on her return. 'There are soldiers everywhere.'

'What do you mean?' This time it was Frau Bucker who was the first to ask.

'It looks like they are setting something up at the tower. I could see boxes at the base and some soldiers were unloading their jeeps. There is total chaos up there, as you can imagine, teachers running around like headless chickens, back and forth pointing and arguing with the soldiers. I heard one teacher say he wants to speak to the Officer in charge. Sorry I don't know any more. I rushed back to tell you.'

'I wonder what sort of soldiers these are,' said Maria.

'They are from our Garrison in town. I recognised some of them,' Hannelore replied.

'Hannelore, do you think you could go back and find out more?' we all looked at Frau Bucker when she asked this question.

'Well, I have smelled Hilde's cheesecake all day now and if there is no School Fete here today we could go home and eat it ourselves.' she continued. 'Of course I will go and find out. I will try not to be too long.' Hannelore replied.

'We come,' said Klaus and Hugo as one. 'But only if you take my hand' she told them.

Before Renate could say anything I bent down and whispered, 'Will you hold Mamma's hand, so that Mamma does not get lost?' she accepted that explanation.

The soldiers and the school teachers eventually came to an agreement. The commissioning of the tower, as a Military Air Defence Post, had been planned and approved for the following day. What had not been made clear to the headmaster was, the setting up would be done one day in advance.

The soldiers moved all their equipment back into their vehicles and helped with setting up the School Fete.

Frau Bucker kept a watchful eye on Hannelore who seemed engrossed in conversations with young soldiers. That was in between taking big bites out of the cheesecake, which after all, she had smelled all day.

The children were very tired when we finally got back home and soon sound asleep in their beds. Just before I had time to settle in front of the radio to listen to Radio 21.57 hour's closing song of Lili Marlene in the happy knowledge that my Karl was listening too.

Chapter 38

After almost exactly one year in Africa, Karl was back home in January 1942. He was wounded. A shoulder injury, not inflicted during combat but instead it was a freak accident. The jeep he was travelling in hit a rock and turned upside down. The driver had several broken ribs and one of his legs was badly damaged. He was flown to a hospital in Italy.

Karl's shoulder had healed well but he was told to keep his arm in a sling. I was just happy he was alright, that nothing more serious had happened and that he was home. He did not have to report back for two months. I could not remember spending a whole two months together since the beginning of the War.

None of the letters I wrote to him had been passed on but I expected that. We would go through the diary which I had kept up.

Klaus was the only one of the children who recognised him. Every time Renate saw him she hid behind me and when Karl tried to coax her to come and see her Pappa, she would run away. Karl was worried that she had hardly grown since he saw her last and wanted to see the doctors there and then but we could not get an appointment for two weeks. Karl-Heinz toddled curiously towards Karl every time he was asked.

When Karl wanted to see his parents he hoped I would go as well. I said yes. Although nobody had been back to visit the children, which must have been nearly two years ago by then, they had kept in regular contact, never forgetting one of the children's birthdays or Christmas.

He arranged the transport. We were sent a small lorry, but it did have tarpaulin on the top to keep out the cold, plus they had put blankets inside for the children. It was unusually mild for the middle of January, otherwise I think I would have declined. We took a couple of suitcases with everything we would need for the two nights we would be staying.

When we were helped by some soldiers to climb up onto the back of the lorry, a shiver went right through me. I had just pictured Harel and his family, being loaded like cattle and transported away.

'Hilde, what are you doing? We are waiting to go,' Karl asked me, after I had decided I could not do this and started to climb back down.

'Mamma, come,' Klaus reached out his hand and he looked so full of expectation, I knew I could not back out.

I had forgotten how large the house was and the land surrounding it. The children marvelled at the sight of the horses and wanted to run over immediately to stroke them, except Renate, who had reverted back into being shy. To my surprise my father-in-law stepped forward, crouched down and produced a small doll he had hidden behind his back and said: 'This dolly is lost and is afraid, do you think you could look after her?'

Of course she could.

There were cakes and hot drinks when we arrived. To my embarrassment the children wolfed them down, like I had not given them anything to eat for days. Just as well because none of them liked their dinner of cabbage soup and bread, they did not even try it, it was the smell which put them off.

'You should teach your children to eat their food, they cannot just live off cake. They must learn to eat what is given to them.' Karl's mother said to him, challengingly.

To my delight he replied, 'I wish you had checked with us, Klaus is not allowed cabbage and Renate and Karl-Heinz have come out in sympathy,' he lied, winking at me. 'If we can make some porridge for now that would be fine,' he added. 'You did get some milk?'

I hoped Renate would not wet her bed tonight. If she did, that would just make this evening complete.

After the meal, Karl and his father retired with a glass of brandy to a separate room, whilst I helped to clear up the dishes, trying to make polite conversation with his mother. She told me Gertrud got married the previous year. Her husband was a schoolteacher. I immediately thought of Frank. I must ring him to find out how

119

everybody was in Berlin, something I had neglected to do and now regretted.

I was relieved when we joined Karl and his father. We had heard them arguing for the last five minutes. Even Karl's mother looked surprised when we heard raised voices.

Whatever the debate was, the two finished as soon as we entered. Karl clearly seemed uncomfortable and flustered. The relief on his face was obvious as soon as he set eyes on me.

Late at night, in bed, I asked him, 'What was the argument with your father all about?'

'Let's just say, I don't agree with some of his views. I think we should cut our visit short and go home tomorrow. Do you mind?'

Did I mind?

Chapter 39

Ursula was born at the beginning of October 1942. My friends were starting to make fun of me and would say things like: 'I see, Karl visits you once a year in the winter.' Or, 'you two have been busy.' But all in all they were as supportive as ever.

This had not been an easy pregnancy and I was very tired most of the time. Food was now rationed. We heard the following announcement repeated over and over again:

'We all have to help with the War effort and certain sacrifices will have to be made. It has to be understood by everybody that the food supply to our brave troops has to be paramount and for this reason it is regrettable but necessary to ration certain foods. Information on which food items are affected will be found at your Town Hall together with a list of coupon distribution centres. Lists will be updated on a regular basis. Take the coupons to your local stores and hand them over together with your payment. Women with little children and pregnant women get extra coupons issued by the health authority.'

At first, queues for the coupons were shambolic, but as soon as the authorities sent some of their SS soldiers, people started to form an orderly line. It was no different at the doctor's office for the additional mother and babies stamps. If anything it was worse. Sometimes we had to wait for hours because nobody could see us until all the patients had been treated.

On my third or fourth visit there, I fainted. I had been up all night with my new baby, which was now fast asleep in her pram. Karl-Heinz not yet two years old had to walk, how else could I take him? Klaus, Renate and Hugo stayed with Frau Bucker. Maria and I made a point of arranging our time, so that we could go to these places together.

Maria screamed when I fell forward and the doctor's door flew open. He had known me for five years, had looked after me, Karl and the children and he also knew Maria, Egon and their children. From the day I fainted, we no longer needed to stay in line but our allocations were waiting for us at the reception. All we had to do was sign for them.

I kept on writing letters in the hope Karl would receive them and I had not heard a word from him. Our own radio broadcasts gave us very little information, if any. I think most people had got tired of the constant propaganda. From the BBC we heard about the bombing raids by the German Luftwaffe in England. From the German Broadcast we heard about the bombing of the American Air Force in Cologne.

Erika coped as best as she could. She had to keep the family at home in a positive mood, which was not easy. Almost four years had passed since Arno disappeared. Herbert and Helmut were now in the Army and Erika was sure that at least one of them was near Stalingrad. Our father had become totally withdrawn, back to his depression days which I remembered well. Only this time it was worse. He had episodes where he would imagine seeing people and having conversations with them. After these conversations he would rock back and forth for hours on end. At other times he would accuse my mother of trying to poison him. He would take a plate and throw it against the wall.

'A waste of good food,' Erika said.

Our mother was having a very difficult time. Most days Guenter and Traute had to stay at home from school and help to harvest the vegetables and fruit which the family was still growing. She was just too weak to undertake that as well as taking care of the animals. The initial excitement of having Lisbet at home was starting to wear off. Lisbet had not bargained on being a farm worker or a maid at her parents' home. She had been brought up leading a fine pampered life.

Erika said, 'Mind my word, it will not be long now, there will be a letter on the kitchen table and Lisbet will be gone.'

'Good riddance to her,' she then added.

Erika suggested she would stop working and stay and help at home, but my mother was adamant that she was not going to allow Erika to ruin her life. I said a silent prayer and a thank you to my mother for that.

'I wish we could get some help on our farm' she said. 'Any idea what we could do?' she asked me.

I had to admit, I did not know and changed the subject. 'Have you heard from Erich?' She had, the good news was he had come back from Russia and was now deployed to France. Before he left, the two of them had become secretly engaged.

'Why did you not tell me that straight away?'

Instead of replying she asked, 'Have you spoken to Frank lately?'

I told her I had tried but the school had simply told me he was not there. When I asked them when he would be back, they said they didn't know and just hung up.

'Has mother not heard from Helene recently?' I then asked.

'No, not a word and she is getting quite anxious.'

'Tell our mother I am trying to go to Berlin to go and see them.'

'Will you?' she could not believe what I just said.

I could not believe it either, but I think that is something I should have done a long time ago. 'I will check whether I can get a ticket. If I get a connection from Hannover it would only take about three and half hours from there.'

Chapter 40

November1942
Lehrter Bahnhof ,Berlin

I had always marvelled at this station. Especially today arriving late afternoon at sunset as the golden rays lit up the roof like the pot of gold at the end of a rainbow. I had to stop and take it all in. I would just like to stand there for a while. Excitement had run over me, like a wave when the tide comes in, as soon as the train reached the outskirts of Berlin.

I had a seat by the window. The soldier next to me moved across as far as he could so that I had space for the pram and my little suitcase. Two women with a boy of about four years old sat opposite. Ursula was quiet most of the way but I needed to breastfeed her once. The soldier said he would have a cigarette outside the carriage apartment in the corridor and I pulled the curtain across.

Outside the station I had my back to the river Spree. I shivered when the memories of the night I almost drowned myself came back to me. I forced myself to turn around to look at the river. It had a slight covering of ice, not yet completely frozen over, very similar to that night so many years ago. I smiled. The river looked peaceful now, not threatening at all. Instead it had a calming effect and I was glad to be alive.

The train journey had taken me through *Braunschweig, Magdeburg* and *Potsdam* before reaching *Charlottenburg* where I nearly stood up, if the curious looks of my fellow passengers had not stopped me in my tracks. I strained my neck, trying to see the street I used to live in with Frau von Buelow and wondered what had happened to her and the kind footman Herr Ludwig.

Outside the station I needed to find a place to change Ursula into some clean clothes. Frau Bucker had made me some nappies out of old bed sheets, with strict instructions to throw away the soiled ones. 'No need to arrive with a smelly little Ursula at your sister's house' she insisted.

Maria gave me an address of a nurse she knew in Berlin just in case there was nobody at home at Helene and Frank's apartment. *Alexander Platz* was not far from the train station, only a couple of stops via the *S- Bahn*. Ursula was wrapped up warm and asleep in her pram, there was no need to disturb her now. I was sure I would be able to attend to her somewhere there, even if it meant using the public facilities.

I spotted Harel's old café from the distance. From where I stood it looked the same. The pain of what had happened to him, Karina and their family since I saw them last almost ten years ago, took my breath away and tears started to form in my eyes. Two elderly women, both wearing long grey coats, black scarves around their heads and black gloves, walked towards me and stopped. Only then did I see the yellow star with the word *Jude* at the left side of their coat.

'Are you alright?' one of them asked me.

'The café over there, is it still open?'

Both looked at me and when they did not reply I continued, 'I used to come here all the time, almost ten years ago now. Friends of mine used to own it, Harel and Karina, did you know them?'

'Harel and Karina left a long time ago, a new owner runs it now. Yes it is open.' 'For some people.' added the other woman.

I walked over and looked through the window. Things had changed inside. The coffee bar had been replaced plus new tables and chairs. The colour of the walls was now a soft blue. Where the pictures of Polish and East Prussian towns had been, there now hung photos of the *Fuehrer*, on his own, or pictures of parades with hundreds of soldiers marching, Hitler on a balcony and the soldiers arms raised in the Hitler salute. I recognised some photos of the Olympic stadium I had seen in the newspaper.

A young couple walked past me. 'Excuse me, Fraulein,' said the man and opened the door. I then noticed the sign at the door "*NO JEWISH*". Familiar sounds drifted through the opening, followed by

'*Heil Hitler*'. It felt like a knife had just stabbed me through my heart. Ursula stirred and started to cry, as if she felt my pain.

I used the public facilities to make her presentable before we went to look for Helene's apartment. We found it easily enough, although I had never been there before. From the letter boxes in the entrance hall I could see their apartment was on the second floor. A pushchair was left downstairs. I felt I could leave the pram next to it and carried Ursula and my suitcase upstairs. Halfway up I could hear the voices of children. I looked up and saw a little face peering down at me through the railing. When the child spotted me it pulled away, ran back and I heard a door slam.

The nameplate outside the big wooden door said *Endler*. I put my case down and pushed the button on the bell and heard it ringing inside. Whispered voices came through a little open latch which was about hip high. I bent down and said, 'Is your Mamma at home?'

The children quickly scattered and I was greeted with silence. Ursula was protesting in my arms. The only thing I could do was to sit on the staircase and wait.

A door on the opposite side opened slightly and an old woman starred at me.

'Do you know when Frau Endler will be back? 'I quickly added, 'I am her sister and I am here to visit her for a few days.' I had learned some time ago that nobody would give you any information of any kind unless they were convinced you were who you claimed to be. I was not surprised that she just shut the door.

'Mamma has gone shopping,' I now heard through the gab. The voice of a young girl. Giggles of more children behind her.

I heard the door open downstairs then a turn of a key at the letter box, followed by heavy footsteps. A woman's head appeared, covered by a floral patterned scarf, a fur collared coat, with two shopping bags, one in each hand. The head was bending down, although I instinctively knew it was Helene. I did not recognise her. A shallow lifeless face looked up. Her coat swamped her thin frame. The same coat she wore so proudly that day in Berlin when she introduced me to Frank. She looked at me, dropped her bags and covered her mouth with both hands.

126

'Oh, my God! Hilde! What are you doing here? 'Behind me the door flew open and three little children peered at me: a tall girl about eight years old; two boys: one about five and one about three years old. 'Mamma, who is that?' the girl asked.

'Dorothy, take Aunt Hilde's case.'

Frank had been drafted several months ago. Helene knew he was deployed to Russia and had not heard from him since he left. He had a big argument at his school. His teaching plan was going to change - geography in the old way was no longer taught. His lessons were now going to be of a political agenda with the view that Germany was reclaiming countries which were rightfully theirs. Frank's open socialist views had been frowned on by the authority before, but when he flatly refused to follow the new instruction it had cost him his job. A week later his army papers arrived.

The school would not pay his wages, claiming he was dismissed because of insubordination.

The Army Office claimed, they needed the paperwork from the school to pay her the soldier's pay. As far as they knew nothing could be done until then, and even if she had the right papers it would take some time. Helene scraped by. She cleaned a couple of offices late afternoon and early evening. Dorothy looked after her little brothers. They knew not to open their apartment door or speak to strangers.

The next day we walked Dorothy to school and told her to go straight home at lunchtime. The neighbour had agreed to let her wait at her apartment until we returned. We had planned to spend the whole day trying to solve the problem between the school and the Army office.

The Principal would not see us claiming to be busy.

'You wait here and look after your boys. I will take Ursula and find his office.' With that I stood up. Although my sister was older than me, I had the feeling she had not learned to fight for herself and her children.

I opened the office door and a stern-looking secretary jumped up from her chair behind a large desk. A coffee cup was knocked over, spilling its light brown liquid over some papers. She grabbed the spoiled sheets, lifted them up and tried to shake the coffee onto the floor with little success, before she turned and faced me.

'You cannot come in here!' she shouted. 'You have already been told the Principal is not available, try again tomorrow.'

'Frau,' I started to say, 'Sorry, I don't know your name. I have plenty of time today. I will just sit here and wait. You don't mind if I feed my little girl, while I am here, do you?' With that I undid the buttons of my coat.

'Wait, wait I will see if he is free now.' I could see she was flustered. She opened a door half covered with frosted class on which 'Principal's Office' was stencilled.

He protested strongly. Listening to him, Frank must have been the worst teacher they had at the school as far as he remembered. I quietly wondered why in that case he had been promoted to Form Teacher only the year before.

We got our letter from the school, but by now it was already afternoon, too late to go to the Army office today.

'Let's go to Café Kranzler.' I suggested. By now Helene was in high spirits and would agree to anything. The café was full. I sensed a sigh of relief coming from my sister and knew she was going to change her mind. I noticed she had checked the prices from the list at the window.

I saw some people vacate a large table in the corner and simply went inside, giving Helene no chance to walk away. I ordered for all of us, plus a cake to take away for Dorothy, thinking back to the last time I was here. That afternoon I had met Helene and her then fiancé Frank, hoping he would pick up my bill that day. It was a wonderful feeling that although it was only a small gesture I could do something for my sister and her family.

Chapter 41

My mother told me the exact circumstances of my father's death in a long letter I received early in 1943. Erika had already broken the news to me on the telephone and said that my mother could not bring herself to speak to me but would write instead.

My father had lost his balance on the railway line which he and his workmates were checking for damage after the recent frost. He tried to break his fall but landed on the shoulder on the same side as his amputated arm. The wound was substantial although not life-threatening. That was until the infection set in. The doctor told my mother that there was nothing that could be done for my father, he did not even have enough antiseptic to clean the wound. My father died a week later of septicaemia.

By the time I heard about his death my father was already buried at the small cemetery not far from where we lived. The same cemetery where we had buried our cousin Norbert after he fell through the ice so many years ago. It was unusual for my mother to pour her heart out to me, but she also told me that Lisbet was thinking of returning to her husband. She had left him in her pursuit to live with her long-lost family. I could not believe my mother actually wrote what she thought:

'I asked Lisbet to help with the cleaning and washing also with the farming in the Spring. Hilde, I just can't do it anymore. Traute and Guenter are really trying, but they are still so young. Traute is refusing to go to school. Grete is working at the department store as a sales assistant. She is such a good girl, every week she puts the money on the kitchen table. I make sure she keeps a little for herself. But Lisbet is far too good for hard work. She actually said so and flew into a rage, accusing me of first giving her away and when she found us, I treat her like my servant. Oh, Hilde, I wished we could find someone to help, if we don't, we have to give up our farm and

go and live in town, but who would want to buy it in such uncertain times ?

I felt her despair running through every one of her words. She never mentioned my brothers Arno, Helmut or Herbert, but I knew from Erika, that there had been no news.

With my mother's letter came also a short note from Oleg.

Ludmilla's father was gone. Gone was the word he used. I tried not to think of what that meant. Most of their friends now had to wear the yellow stars on their coats. Almost every day somebody else went missing. Ludmilla's friends hid wherever they could as soon as they heard Military vehicles arriving. Nobody switched any lights on in their apartments at night and curtains remained firmly closed. Neighbours got together and developed a look out and warning system. The children coped, but were confused. The school friends they walked with every morning, did not return the following day. Oleg did not know how to explain or what to tell them. The children were no longer allowed outside on their own. As always Oleg finished his letter with: *'Pray for us'*

Chapter 42

21st March 1943, the first day of Spring. The War in North Africa, as far as we were concerned, was over. Field Marshal Rommel was back in Germany. The years on the African Continent and the battles they fought had taken a toll on his health. Karl told me the Field Marshal was physically and mentally exhausted and had been recalled.

Karl had returned ten days ago. I almost did not recognise him. A thin lifeless man stood outside my front door. His dark coat was open and underneath he was wearing a khaki- coloured shirt covered with, what looked like, a lightweight jacket with matching shorts. He took his field cap off and dropped it on the floor. 'Don't let me in Fraulein Hilde,' he said.

I rushed forward and he took a step back, holding up his hands up in defence and continued 'No! Hilde, don't touch me!'

Only now did I see head lice crawling all the way down his neck, feeding on the scab covered scars on his forehead. I took a tentative step towards him, the stench almost made me gag. But it was my Karl who stood there and he needed me this minute more than ever.

Klaus and Renate had heard voices at the front door and came rushing out. I just managed to grab them by their arms to stop them.

'Mamma, it is Pappa?' protested Klaus.

'Yes, it is, but your Pappa is not very well. You must not touch him right now. Please go to Frau Bucker and ask her to come.'

'Is Pappa not well like Renate was when she was a baby, does he have to go into isolation?'

'No, your Pappa just needs some medication and then some rest.'

Karl turned around and looked at the staircase behind him and asked 'There is a little boy sitting there, is he one of ours?'

I knew my tears were exactly what he did not need right now, but I could not stop them. 'Yes Karl, it is Karl-Heinz, he is nearly three and a half years old.' Karl-Heinz looked at me at the mention of his name, stared at the stranger in front of him, panicked and stood up.

'Come inside Karl-Heinz, go with Renate and play in your room.'

When Karl-Heinz was next to Karl, he stretched his little hand out to touch the man standing there at our front door. 'No!', Karl and I shouted together. Poor Karl-Heinz soiled his trousers there and then.

Frau Bucker had witnessed the scene unfolding in front of her from the top steps, Klaus was right behind her. One of her hands covered her mouth, stopping her from crying out.

'Klaus, get Hannelore, and if Hannelore is not there get her Grandmother, we need to boil plenty of hot water, downstairs in the washroom. Ask her for any alcohol she might have. Do you know where I keep my bottle of brandy?' Klaus nodded. 'Please go and get it, but be careful not to drop it. Hilde, do you have any oil, any type of oil in the house?' I nodded yes.

Frau Bucker must have been a school teacher once, the way she took control of the situation and issued instructions.

Karl had still not moved. 'Karl, can you make it downstairs?' She asked him very softly. He started to turn around to go towards the cellar where the wash room was. 'You have to take all of your clothes off and leave them on the floor.' she continued.

'All of them?' I asked.

'Hilde, bring Karl a sheet, he can cover himself with it.'

Hannelore and her Grandmother had now joined us. 'Thank God you are here.' Frau Bucker turned to them. 'Hannelore, tell all the neighbours not to use the washroom today. When they ask you why, tell them the truth, Karl is back and needs a good clean.'

In the washroom, Karl told me to burn all his clothes in the furnace.

'What about the uniform?' I asked. 'Yes, the uniform as well. Especially the uniform,' he insisted.

I shaved Karl's entire body and then covered it with oil in the hope that this would kill off any remaining lice and their eggs. He soaked in the bath for a very long time, Hannelore's Grandmother kept the supply of hot water coming as fast as she could. Finally, I rubbed her last bottle of Vodka over his head and body, this should help to prevent any infections. At some stage Hannelore took all four children off to find Maria.

At last Karl was in bed asleep. We had talked very little during the clean-up. I knew my Karl, knew he felt ashamed.

Maria arrived just as I said 'We did not use any of your brandy, Frau Bucker.'

'Good.' she replied, 'get the glasses.'

Chapter 43

'My dark blue dress, the one with the lace collar. Do you think it would be suitable for such a grand event?' I asked Maria, whilst going through my wardrobe.

'The one Frau Lehmann gave you? That sounds perfect, let's have a look.'

I took the dress from the shelf. I had folded it using some old fabric and mothballs to keep it from getting damaged. I had never thought of any occasion where I could wear it.

'Do you think it will still fit me?' I laid it out on the bed and touched the fabric, dark blue silk organza, which lay over a satin underdress, winged short sleeves. It looked a little bit outdated, but then what did I know about fashion. I had never been to a Ball before.

'Put it on, Hilde, let's find out.'

It was quiet in the apartment. Karl had taken the children out. Klaus had started school just after Easter and was proud his father would walk him there, even though he had to hold hands with his younger sister, whilst his father pushed Ursula's pram helped by Karl-Heinz.

Karl-Heinz was still wary of his father. He could not get used to having him around and his mother was now sharing her room with somebody he had never met before.

Karl had been subdued since he had come home. By now it was the middle of May and I had hoped his recovery would have been faster.

When the invitation to attend a Grande Ball in Goslar, in honour of Field Marshal Rommel, arrived in the post, Karl's mood changed dramatically. His old enthusiasm returned. He started to plan how we would get there, inquired about a room for the night. He ordered and paid for an Officer's dress uniform.

Maria, as always, volunteered to look after our children.

'Are you sure you can cope, we will be away for two nights?' I asked her again for the second time this morning.

'Hilde, stop worrying. It is not that I have to look after them all on my own, is it? Inge took some time off. Hugo and Klaus will be at school most of the day. Plus you never know, you might meet the Field Marshal himself.' Maria could be very persuasive.

'Just to get a glimpse of him would be really lovely,' I admitted, pulling the satin over my head. It finished half way up my calf. Maria closed the zip on the side and helped me with the organza layer. This layer was slightly longer, nearly touching my ankles. It was fastened at the back with twenty small buttons, covered in the same fabric.

Maria stepped back to look at her handy work but did not say anything.

'What, what does it look like?' I asked her.

'You look wonderful, Hilde, look for yourself, ' she replied and turned me round to face the mirror.

The person in the mirror looking at me, must have been somebody else. That person was wearing the most beautiful dress but I looked down at the shoes. 'I don't have any shoes which would go with it, Maria, and no small bag and look at my hair. I cannot go. I would embarrass Karl,' I said and sat down on the bed and felt sorry for myself. 'Besides, the dress is creased and stinks of mothballs.'

'Salty tears on the delicate fabric will not help.' She looked at me crossly. 'We will go to the black market tomorrow and find you some shoes. I have a small bag and we can get your hair cut. Anyway it is about time you started looking a bit more fashionable. What do you think?' she added.

'I think the dress still smells and I wonder what small bag YOU have which would be suitable?' I looked at her and we both started laughing.

Chapter 44

A car was sent to pick us up from Hotel Achterman shortly after 19.00 hours. We had arrived in Goslar about mid-day. It was only a short drive to the Imperial Palace and the Grande Ball was going to begin at 20.00 hours with a festive dinner followed by speeches and dancing. We all had to be at our allocated place before the evening would officially begin.

A queue of cars were in front of us. I looked at the other women arriving and was thankful Hannelore's Grandmother had lent me a silk stole. It really complemented my dress, which by now was no longer creased or ill-smelling.

My car door was opened by a young soldier who reached for my hand to help me out. Once through the doors of the Palace we were greeted by the Master of Ceremonies. A second soldier took our invitation and handed it to him. He announced us 'Officer Paekel and his wife Hilde.'

I hoped my legs would stop shaking when we descended the large staircase, leading into a big hall below. I had linked my arm with Karl's who seemed totally at ease. One soldier took my stole and another offered us a glass of champagne. I looked at Karl to see whether I should accept one, but Karl had already taken two glasses and handed me mine with a smile. 'To a lovely evening Fraulein Hilde,' he said and touched my glass with his.

'Let's see where our table is and who we are sitting with,' he continued and we went over to a large board with table numbers and names written on it. Several officers and their wives were there already and I was surprised at how many people Karl knew.

Our table was near the front and we would have a good view of the head table, the band behind and the podium. The table had been set for eight people. I recognised one of the officers from our time in Goslar, but I did not know his wife. We were the last to arrive and found our place setting. I was going to sit opposite the officer I remembered and Karl opposite his wife. I had promised Maria I would tell her every detail of the evening. Eager not to forget anything I tried to scrutinise the table decorations out of the corner of my eye.

Very delicate flower arrangements, little lilies of the valley interlinked with small white silk ribbons. Silver candelabras with white tall candles. White damask tablecloth and napkins.

Three different sized crystal glasses at each place, silver knives and forks, the first knife for each setting was a fish knife.

I had never been as grateful to Frau von Buelow as at this precise moment. I had arranged many dinner parties at her house, some of them for famous people, this table in all its glory did not faze me.

Only now I noticed that the whole room was decorated in the same colours, green and white, with similar but larger flowers and large ribbons.

'Hilde, Hilde?' it was Karl calling me. I had been so engrossed in my observations I did not realise that I had been asked a question by the female guest standing next to me.

'I'm really sorry, I was just thinking about the children,' I used as an excuse.

'You and me, both' she said smiling. 'Who is looking after them?'

Before I knew it we were swapping baby stories.

The arrival of the main guests who would be sitting at the head table was announced by a fanfare. We all stood behind our seats, waiting. My heart beat so loud I was sure even the band up on the stage could hear it. I tried not to stretch my neck to have a better look, in case it was considered unladylike. Karl took my hand and gave me a reassuring smile. It had the right effect, I started to calm down. There must have been over a dozen Officers in various dress uniforms marching in. Every one of them stood behind a chair and the one in the middle remained empty.

Disappointment swept over me, the Field Marshal was not going to be here.

'Ladies and Gentlemen, Officers, please welcome our guest tonight, Field Marshal Erwin Rommel.' The fanfare started again followed by a drum roll. And there he was. The Field Marshal, walking proudly, acknowledging people at the tables before greeting the officers who would be sitting beside him and who had begun applauding as soon as the Field Marshal was announced. Field Marshal Rommel was trying to speak but was drowned out by the applause which did not stop. Finally he indicated with his hands 'enough' and when the room grew quiet he said:

'Ladies, Officers, thank you for inviting me to spend the evening with you. I owe a great deal to many of you here, and it makes me happy to see so many smiling faces .Please sit down, enjoy your meal and have a lovely evening.'

We all sat down and the first course was served: smoked herring filets with a parsley sauce, accompanied by a glass of white wine. The band played softly in the background and our table was engrossed with lively conversation.

'I think he just looked at us' said the officer's wife who I had talked to before, during our main course of pheasant, potatoes and red cabbage.

'Who?' I asked.

'The Field Marshal, but don't look now otherwise he will know we are staring at him.'

'I have not been staring at him, but I am very tempted,' I replied, now smiling at her.

A selection of small pieces of cake, served with Tokaj wine, rounded off the meal. The food was delicious, and delicate, perfectly cooked, I thought, thinking back to the times I had to present meals similar to this one.

After all the plates were cleared away, the officer next to the Field Marshal stood up to make a speech. To my astonishment it was very brief and free of propaganda.

He thanked the Field Marshal for accepting the invitation and taking the time out of a busy schedule to come and join his officers and their wives this evening to give support and thanks to our brave soldiers and their commanders. He continued by saying, 'I would now like to ask Field Marshal Rommel to officially open the Grande Ball with the first dance.'

Karl stood up, pulled my chair back, and offered me his arm. He looked so handsome in his dress uniform and I had noticed several women looking at him throughout the evening.

Everybody went towards the dance floor and standing on one side, facing the head table and the band.

The Field Marshal rose, and soft murmuring went through the crowd as he stepped forward towards where everybody gathered. We were right in front. 'He is very tall,' I whispered to Karl. Karl squeezed my arm slightly, looked down into my face and I could see a sparkle in his bright blue eyes.

The Field Marshal walked slowly, greeting people on the way, shaking hands, exchanging words. By now I could almost hear what was said, he was so close. I wanted to look around to try and work out where he was heading but could not take my eyes off him.

He stopped right in front of us. 'Karl, it is good to see you,' he stretched out his hand, took Karl's and shook it.

'Field Marshal, may I introduce my wife, Hilde,' Karl replied.

'It is an honour to meet you, Hilde.' He took my outstretched hand in both of his and held it.

All I could think of at that moment was, I wish I had taken my gloves with me, I would never wash them again and I would keep them forever. 'Field Marshal, the honour is mine' I replied.

He took a bow towards me and said, 'May I have this dance, Hilde?' He looked at Karl who nodded and let go of my arm.

I felt the heat rising in my face, felt the eyes of every woman in the room burning at my back. I accepted his arm and we went to the middle of the dance floor. He nodded to the band, which started playing. The Field Marshal took my hand and put his right hand softly on my back, then he started to lead me into a slow waltz.

He made it seem so easy, after the first few steps he said, 'I have heard a lot about you, Hilde.'

'You have?' I stammered.

'Karl never stops talking about you,' he continued.

'Karl talks about me?' I must have sounded like an idiot.

He had a disarming smile when he said, 'Oh, yes, all the time, about you and his three children.'

I finally found my voice. 'We have four now, Field Marshal. Ursula was born last October.'

He laughed. 'That must have been a surprise when he got back.'

'Yes, it was.' By now I had forgotten all the other people still standing there, not moving until they were told to do so.

'Hilde, if there is ever anything I can do for you, please do not hesitate to ask.'

He saw the shock in my face and continued, 'Really Hilde, anything.'

I was taken aback for a few seconds then looked directly into his eyes and said. 'There is something Field Marshal.'

'What would that be, Hilde?' Now his eyes were searching my face.

'I have a friend, he and his family live in Poland, about 30 km west of Warsaw.' I stopped there. Field Marshal Rommel had raised his eyebrows in surprise. He was just going to answer but he must have thought better of it and nodded at me instead. I took that as a sign to continue.

'He has an agricultural food distribution centre there. But he needs to have the right paperwork for him, his wife Ludmilla and their children to travel to my mother in Titlist, to stay there and work the farm. He needs the working permit as well. His Name is Oleg Lorenz. The town is Sierakow and the name of his Company is O. Lorenz and Son, Distribution.'

There was no stopping me now. The words just rushed out of me. I did not know what made me take this chance. It was as if it had been building up inside me for a long time. I still looked at the Field Marshal's face, bit my lip and said, 'I am so sorry. I should not have said anything.'

Field Marshal Rommel nodded again, encouraging me. 'His name and town, is that enough?' I continued.

The music stopped, I stood there frozen and was brought back by the applause. The Field Marshal offered me his arm again and walked me back to Karl.

'Thank you for the dance, Hilde. Thank you Karl,' gave a short bow, turned round and walked away.

140

I was shaking when Karl and I joined the dance floor. The Field Marshal had gone back to his table. I kept looking over and I saw that one of the soldiers handed something to him which seemed to be a pen. The Field Marshal then wrote something on his napkin, folded it, looked in my direction, nodded and put it into his uniform pocket.

Chapter 45

'Tell us again, from the beginning, from the minute you arrived at Hotel Achtermann!' Inge and Hannelore wanted to hear the story again. They still could not believe what had happened that evening. But today I had a surprise for them. In the post I had received a photograph. It had been passed on from the Organiser of the Grande Ball. It was a picture just of me with Field Marshal Rommel on the dance floor.

The photograph was taken from the side and you could clearly see who I was dancing with. I had not yet shown it to Maria, who sat on one of my kitchen chairs, clutching her latest letter from Egon. He had been a Prisoner of War in England for over two years now and his letters contained nothing but optimism. He heard the English news broadcasts every day, he said. But he did not mention anything about its content. He knew, if he did, the letters would be censored or may not even be forwarded on. But indirectly Maria understood that he wanted her to listen to them as well, as often as she could.

'Go on, Hilde, tell us again,' Maria now said. She and Frau Bucker knew what I had said to the Field Marshal during our dance. Nobody else knew, not even Karl. Karl had not asked me what I talked about, or whether I talked at all. I was grateful for that because I did not want to have to lie to my husband, it was hard enough to feel I had to keep something from him at all.

'Let's wait for Frau Bucker to come downstairs. Ah, Hannelore, your god-son wants you.' Karl-Heinz had come into the kitchen and climbed on her lap. A little ping of jealously went through me, he had no problem bonding with Hannelore, I thought, but immediately felt guilty about it.

When everybody was in the kitchen, drinking fake coffee and eating real home-made apple strudel, I said, 'Oh, this came in the post today,' and laid the picture in the middle of the table.

As expected Maria was the first to grab it. 'What is that?' she asked, followed by, 'Oh, my God! Hilde, that is fantastic, where did you get it from?'

Now everybody stretched their hands out to take the photo at the same time.

Chapter 46

Norway! I had long given up asking Karl why? Three weeks after the Grande Ball he got the news he was going to Norway.

'You know I am an excellent skier,' he tried to make a light-hearted conversation of the fact he was leaving again. 'Norway is not that far away and I have been told I will only be there for a few months. All I will have to do is to control the borders.'

'You are going from one extreme to the other,' I said. 'From the heat in Africa to the snow in Norway.'

'I don't think they have quite worked out what to do with me right now. Field Marshal Rommel is still to be given a new assignment. I think he is not well enough yet.

'And you think you are, do you?' I asked. 'You have been home for just over three months and you are pronounced fit and well. I just want it to stop Karl. This is madness!' I raised my voice.

Karl gave me a worried look. 'Please Hilde, don't say these things out loud. There are many people thinking the same. I have seen what can happen to them if somebody overhears and reports it to the Gestapo. Please do not let me worry whilst I am away.'

'Have you heard from him since the Ball?' I now asked

'Who?'

'The Field Marshal,' I said.

'No, not directly, I have not seen him, as far as I know he is at his headquarters in Munich.'

Karl-Heinz had still not formed a strong bond with his father, which started to worry me. Now with Karl away again, I dreaded to think what it would do to their relationship. Karl had really tried, making special effort, trying to spend time just with Karl-Heinz when Klaus was at school and Renate and I would take the pram with Ursula to go and see Maria or do to some food shopping.

Karl-Heinz would go to the children's bedroom and play by himself or just hide in the corner. He would only come out again, when I returned.

Karl and I had talked to the paediatrician about it on one of Renate's check-ups. She told us the best way would be to just let him be and not force it. That would only make it worse. She also thought that leaving Karl-Heinz alone with his father had the opposite effect. He felt he had done something wrong and for punishment was not allowed to go out with his mother and his sisters. Karl cried he felt so sad.

Chapter 47

Maria told me that Erika left a message to phone her the following day just after 13.00 hours. It was Ursula's first birthday 2nd of October 1943 that day and I took her and Karl-Heinz with me. Klaus was at school and I got a place in the Kindergarten for Renate. I knew that at school and at playschool both of my children would be fed and receive hot milk or, in Klaus's case, hot chocolate. Klaus and Hugo were in the same class and had been reprimanded a couple of times so far, always up to something. Maria and I had to go to school and we were told, if things did not settle down, the two boys would be separated. That threat alone calmed them down considerably. Especially my warning to Klaus that I would change the order to milk instead of cocoa.

All the way to Maria's I had taught Ursula to say 'Aunty Erika' loud and clear. Karl-Heinz looked at me hoping he would be allowed to say something as well and I said to him: 'Karl-Heinz, are you going to tell your aunty what noise your toy train makes?'

He beamed at me and said 'Choo Choo' and pulled his arm down in a motion he had seen a train driver do at the railway crossing at the other end of our road.

No sooner had I dialled her number than Erika answered, as if she had been sitting there, staring at the phone, willing it to ring. Instead of 'hello' she said 'Hold on I will pass you to our mother.'

I thought I should have taught Ursula to say 'Omi' as well.
Karl-Heinz was pulling on my skirt. 'Hold on, mother, Karl-Heinz wants to speak to you.' I quickly whispered 'It is Omi' in his ear.

He made all the right train noises and my mother was laughing when it was my turn to get the phone.

We talked about the children and how everybody was when she eventually said: 'Oh, I forgot to tell you, we have help on the farm now, we don't need to sell it and move after all.'

'You have?' I asked.

'Yes a very nice family, they knocked on the door and asked whether we needed somebody to work the land. Yes, very nice indeed. A young man, his wife and their children. Their German is pretty good and I told them to go to the local school to see whether they would accept the children. Oleg and Ludmilla took them this morning.'

I pulled a chair from behind me and sat down, my legs were shaking. My mother chose her words perfectly.

'That is really good news, you now have the extra help you needed,' I replied as calmly as I could.

But there was no stopping my mother now. 'I gave them your old room, I hope you don't mind. Lisbet is sharing with Gisela and Traute, and to my surprise she is happy. Anything is better than to have to do all the housework and the harvests, I presume. She can now go back to being a lady.' The last sentence had a very sad undertone. 'Anyway, I gave Oleg a letter for the school, that should help. I will let you speak to Erika now,' and with that she was gone.

'Wow!' I said to Erika, 'That is good news.'

'There is more,' she replied. 'I have been offered a position in Denmark to work at the Communication Centre in Copenhagen. I was asked a few weeks ago, but said I could not leave home. But now we have the extra 'HELP' (she stressed the word 'HELP') our mother said I should go. What do you think?'

'What about Erich?' I replied.

'I am coming to that, just wait.' Erika continued, 'We are getting married. There, I said it.'

'Married?, not without me you don't.' I replied.

'Don't be silly, Hilde, there is no way you can be here, plus we are getting married next week.'

'What is the urgency?' I asked, getting suspicious.

Erika laughed. 'Not what you think anyway. Erich has to get back to France in a couple of weeks and I am not going to let my good-looking fiancé set his eyes on all those French women, not without a wedding ring, I can tell you. Plus, being married I can keep a closer eye on him from the Communication Centre,' she now laughed.

147

'Erika, I am so happy for you and thinking that you are not that far away, only just over 300 km instead 1000 km, is a great feeling. We will have our celebration together when we manage see each other.

Until it was time to collect the boys from school, Maria and I, we went over the telephone conversation again and again.

Chapter 48

Klaus's happiness about hot cocoa at school was short lived. We were now issued ration cards every two weeks and I would have to give all our cocoa coupons to the school in order for him to have these drinks. The same did not apply to milk. This would have meant my other children would have missed out on this treat. He did not understand why I could not do that and I settled it by assuring him they could all have some each night before going to bed.

Until now essential items such as potatoes had not been rationed but they were now. Some other items, such as bread, flour, fat, meat, cheese, had the ration portions cut.

We were advised that local fruit and vegetables were still available without coupons. I tried to work out which fruit would still be growing in the winter.

The root vegetable swede was becoming our main source of nourishment. We used it in stews and mixed it with flour to bake bread.

The one item I did not need was a cigarette coupon. I regularly swapped those for butter or, when Karl came back from Norway, for meat. Although Karl could eat at the Garrison when he was on leave, he insisted on spending as much time with his family as possible.

Instead of eating there, he smuggled some of the food out. On those days it was like a feast of days long-forgotten. Once or twice during his stay we ate in the Officers Mess. Karl was worried how thin I looked but I kept assuring him, there was nothing wrong with me. He did not know how often I went to bed hungry, especially at the end of the two week coupon rations, before being issued with new ones.

Karl soon went away again. Field Marshal Rommel had been appointed Commander in Chief in Italy during August 1943, and that was Karl's next deployment. He left again at the end of November.

I had to go to the black market as I needed extra milk, fat and meat for the children. I had already traded most of my belongings which had some value. I hoped two silver sets of cutlery would get me some of the items I needed. I might be lucky and get some flour as well. I would ask Frau Bucker to bake us all a cake and we could sit together and listen to the radio, as we used to do. I knew Hannelore was at home and Inge would come over later.

Maria had wanted to come with me today but Manfred was not well. She took him to the hospital where Egon's former colleagues would check him over. She would also collect some medicine for Renate which was waiting for me to pick up. Maria would come over to my apartment later.

Karl-Heinz, Ursula in her pram, and I set off to see what we could get. You always had to make sure there were no SS or Gestapo around when you arrived there. It was not that they arrested you for being there, or stopped you from swapping or buying. No, it was worse. They let you make your purchase, hand over your items and/or money and when you walked away, that was when they pounced on you and confiscated everything you just managed to get. Sometimes at the end of the day, they would loot the store-holders as well.

Everything I wanted to bargain with on the days I went, was hidden under Ursula. That way if I spotted somebody, or got a warning, an indication such as a shake of the head from the other people around you, you knew there were Officials watching you. I just looked at the stalls and continued walking. I hoped this would be a better day. I really needed to get some things for the children to eat.

I was in luck, there was nobody around to arouse my suspicion. In fact it seemed unusually quiet. I tried to get the food as quickly as I could and went to a stall holder, who by now recognised me. He did not have everything I needed, but since there were not a lot of customers, he agreed to share the cutlery and extra money with a man, next to him. Whilst those two tried to argue it out, I kept looking nervously over my shoulder. Karl-Heinz was getting bored and started to aggravate Ursula, who protested loudly. The commotion attracted the few people who were still there and started to come over.

'Please,' I said to the store holders, 'My children are hungry. Please hurry!' They must have taken pity on me and handed me everything I had asked for.

Then we heard noises of planes over us and everybody looked up towards the sky.

'Come on, Karl-Heinz, we'd better hurry home. Here, take Mamma's hand.' I decided to take the short-cut over the Town Square, from there it would only be about 20 minutes, if we walked quickly.

It seemed that everybody decided to take the same route. The square was packed with people. I kept pushing on to curious looks of people who had stopped moving.

'Excuse me, I have got to get home.' I said, all the while going forward.

At the front of the queue I came to a stop, the rest of the market had been sealed off. Gestapo and SS were addressing the crowd.

' *This should be an example for you. If you steal from your fellow Germans, you will be severely punished. You all know our Fuehrer will not let his good citizens starve but even though these people decided to help themselves to some of your allocated rations. Go home now and let this be a warning.* ' ' *Heil Hitler.* ' bellowed from some speakers.

Three people: one woman and two elderly men, were swinging by their necks from some make-shift gallows. Each one had a piece of cardboard showing their names tied to their fronts.

Karl-Heinz screamed, and the people near me looked in our direction. I heard one of them saying: 'How can anybody be that heartless and bring her children to a public hanging?'

Chapter 49

The planes, I later learned, were heading for Hamburg. On the way there they dropped leaflets over towns they passed.

We have had leaflet drops before, issued by our own Propaganda Department, telling us how important it was to fight on, and that Germany would be victorious in its struggle to unite the Countries willing to be part of the Third Reich.

But this leaflet drop was different:

'A warning from England and its Allies to the People of Germany. You cannot win this War. We consider the Act of German Warfare a criminal offence and these criminals will be held responsible after their defeat.

We are going to bomb your towns until there is nothing left to fight for. You can stop this now by telling your loved ones to lay down their arms.'

I was still shaking from the shocking event at the main square. Karl-Heinz had completely withdrawn and I hoped Maria would come over soon. I had told Frau Bucker what we witnessed but only after Hannelore went to collect Renate, Klaus and Hugo. Something I had told Maria I would do on my way home from the black market.

'Frau Bucker, I know we have not believed what Goebbels has told us so far but I am really frightened now. How can I protect four little children? I remember what it was like in the First War when I was a little girl, always hiding, always hungry, always afraid. I don't want that for my children and they have seen so much already. Look at Karl-Heinz. Will he ever sleep again?'

'But, Hilde, what can we do? Really, what can we do? Nothing, I tell you, that's what!' said Frau Bucker and she was right of course.

'I wish Karl was here.'

'Karl-Heinz, would you like to help me bake a cake? We can all eat it this afternoon, what do you think?' Frau Bucker now asked him.

He either did not hear, or did not take in what was said to him.

'I think that is a great idea. Karl-Heinz, tell Frau Bucker which cake you like best.'

'Chocolate, that is my best cake,' he said and took Frau Bucker by the hand.

I gave him the tin with the cocoa. 'Hold it really tight, don't let it fall down the stairs.' I hugged him and he was already at the front door,

'Thank you.' I said to Frau Bucker and she took the flour and eggs I had managed to get.

I put the radio on after both had gone upstairs. Ursula was still asleep. She was a really quiet little girl, she only fretted or cried when she was hungry or uncomfortable. Her hair was already long with thick blond curls. She had a lovely shy smile, and saw her big sister Renate as her protector, never leaving her side when she was back from the Kindergarten. Ursula was walking and had started to say a few words. Looking at Ursula in her little cot, I thought 'Nate' was the first word she said. Just shows how little time I had spent with her, I thought regretfully.

'Field Marshal Rommel is making advances in Western France, in preparation of an expected attack by the British and their Allies. Re enforcements are being deployed to secure our position.'

France? Did the radio announcer say France? Maybe I misheard. Surely the Field Marshal was in Italy. That was what Karl told me when he left. If the Field Marshal was in France, then where was Karl?

Chapter 50

Renate proudly carried her 'Cone of Goodies' (*Zuckertuete*) when she started school in the Spring of 1944. A tradition for a long as I can remember. Even I got one on my first day at school back in 1918 during the First War. Now we were fighting a War again and I was determined to make life as pleasant as I possibly could for the children. My mother had never been able to help us. We had to look after ourselves. Like Renate, I was not yet six years old when I started school. I went there on my first day - 5 kilometres through the snow, accompanied only by my brothers.

Renate's 'Cone of Goodies' had taken us a week to make. All the children wanted to help. I found some old cardboard, which we rolled into the cone shape and stuck it together with glue I had made from a water, flour, sugar and vinegar mix. We let it dry overnight to make sure it held together. I did not have crepe paper for the top but used a piece of cloth from an old summer dress. I stitched it to the top and made a string from the same fabric to pull the fabric together to prevent the cone's content falling out. The children decorated it with stickers and her name in big letters.

'This way it will not get lost or be mixed up with somebody else's' Klaus told her.

I had collected and stored little sweet treats to be put into it, plus everybody had contributed something. Inge brought a bag of boiled sweets; Frau Buecker baked some biscuits; the local shop gave me a small colouring book and pencils; Hannelore had knitted a sweater for Renate's favourite doll; Klaus parted with one of his small toy cars, but it took him a while to work out which one he could spare. Karl-Heinz made a drawing. To my amazement he had done our whole family and I had to show him how to put the names above them, including 'Pappa'.

Renate was really worried when I had to take it to the school the day before. At the end of their first day at school each child was called forward to the front, one by one, and with a few encouraging words were handed their cones.

She was fretting all the way there. I had to remind her she was wearing her best dress and shoes.

'Mamma, the shoes are too big, what if I fall over and everybody laughs at me?' 'Mamma, my cardigan itches.' 'Mamma, there is a dirty mark on my dress.' 'Mamma, my socks are falling down.' 'Mamma, my hair clip is coming lose.' She was working herself into a frenzy.

'Nate' I bent down to face her. 'You will be the prettiest, smartest little girl there. You do believe your Mamma, don't you?'

She nodded and held my hand tighter.

I could not believe it was the same girl I collected with Karl-Heinz four hours later. She came skipping down the steps, holding her 'Zuckertuete' in one arm, linking the other arm with another little girl - her new-found friend.

'Mamma, this is Monika, we sit together. Bye, Monika, I will see you tomorrow.'

Monika's mother and I looked at each other with relief.

'My teacher is called Herr Klett' she said. 'He told us about letters and wrote a word on the blackboard and asked whether anybody could read it. I did what you have showed me before. Read every letter carefully in my head: an 'R' an 'A' a 'D' an 'I' and an 'O' and saying it all together slowly in my head, it made the word. I raised my hand and he told me to come forward and I whispered it into his ear. All the other children asked me what it said, but I never told them'.

All the time she was looking at me. I could have burst with pride, but before I could say anything she let go of my hand and ran ahead. 'Pappa, I went to school today.'

There was Karl, standing in the entrance of our apartment block, his rucksack on his back, waving. Renate was in his arms and he lifted her up.

'Karl-Heinz how about you go and greet your Pappa?' I only had to say it once. He bolted towards him. 'Pappa, it's me Karl-Heinz' he shouted. I could see Karl's tears from where I stood taking it all in. 'I know my boy, I know it's my Karl-Heinz.' I heard him say, holding his son close to him.

Chapter 51

Karl gave me a small branch of fresh bay leaves with a promise. He promised one day he would take me to pick my own from a bush just at the bottom of the Monastery in Monte Cassino. He had carried it in his rucksack all the way back.

Later in bed on the first night he was home again, I told him everything that had happened during the last few months, but omitted to say how frightened I now was. I had not kept a copy of the leaflet dropped by the British, but it was imprinted into my memory.

'What do you think it means?' I whispered.

Karl was silent for a while, eventually he said. 'I don't know, Hilde. We have lost a lot of good men in Italy and the Monastery in Monte Cassino is destroyed. I am haunted by the scenes there. I can see the monks running, can hear them chanting and praying. They ran into the middle of the battlefield holding large crosses up towards the sky. Then they stopped right between us and our enemy troops and kneeled down with their rosaries in their hands, like nothing else was going on around them. Totally without fear.'

'I envied them their strength and faith and silently prayed with them. Praying their God would save us all. For a moment there I thought the fighting had stopped. That there was peace, and then it started all over again, only worse this time. Bombs dropping, gunfire from every direction. When the smoke cleared, the monks had gone. Not a trace of them.'

I shivered and moved closer to Karl who reached over and put his arms round me.

'You know I am going to France, don't you?' he then asked. 'I am going to re-join my old Regiment.'

'What is happening, Karl? Where is this all going to end?' I needed to know what he was thinking and continued, 'Is anybody doing anything, anything to put a stop to it?'

'Hilde, it is better that you don't think about it. The less you know the better, trust me on that.'

Chapter 52

6th June 1944

I ran over to Maria's, I wanted her to come to my apartment as soon as she could. I had heard a speech from the US General Eisenhower over the British Broadcast channel, and I wanted her to translate it. It sounded very urgent and I had learned to recognise some English words by now, such as *'defeat' 'allies' ' enemy'' liberation'*.

I realised something major was happening in France, especially since our own German Broadcast issued denials to the effect of:

'Contrary to the statement issued by Britain, our Armies and their Commanders were nowhere taken by surprise. Many British parachute units were wiped out on landing or taken prisoner. Our thoughts are with our brave troops. Heil Hitler.'

When Maria and I got home, Frau Bucker was still sitting in front of the radio. I didn't think she had moved since I left. The sound of the British radio Broadcast was blasting through the rooms. We no longer cared who could hear us.

'It's the King' Maria said.

'What? What, King ?' I was only half-listening to what Maria had just said. I had focussed on Frau Bucker who was sitting there as stiff as a board. 'Frau Bucker, Frau Bucker!' she turned towards me. I let out a sigh of relief. 'We are back Frau Bucker, in a moment we will find out more.'

'The British King, King George VI, he just broadcast a speech to his people,' Maria said, still in her jacket and Manfred still holding her hand.

'What did he say?'

'I only heard part of it. I think he said: *'The British and their Allies face a supreme test,'* and he called on the Nation to pray for the Liberation of Europe.'

159

I went into the kitchen to get Manfred and Karl-Heinz a glass of milk. From the kitchen I heard Maria say, 'Come, Hilde, they are repeating Eisenhower's speech.'

'Soldiers, Sailors and Airmen of the Allied Forces. You are embarking on a great Crusade. The eyes of the World are upon you. Together with our Allies we will bring about the destruction of the German War machine and the end of the Nazi rule, which has terrorised the people of Europe. This will not be an easy task. Our enemy is well equipped and their soldiers are well trained, but the tide has turned and together we march to Victory. God be with you.'

'Frau Bucker? FRAU BUCKER !!!!!!!!'

Chapter 53

'You gave us quite a fright', I said to Frau Bucker, when I took Karl-Heinz and Ursula upstairs. I had made some soup, which I knew she liked and served it with the by now customary bread, made to a large extent with swede. It was astonishing, that although there was not much flour mixed with the root vegetable and shortage of eggs, it managed to look something like the real thing. I had tried to feed her the soup but she was having none of it.

'Hilde, I might have had a heart attack, but that is now over one month ago. I have been discharged and pronounced fit and well, so stop fussing. What are Karl-Heinz and Ursula going to think? A grown-up woman in bed being fed with some, let's have a look at it, some sort of soup.'

'I help' said Karl-Heinz, and climbed on Frau Bucker's bed.

'Yes, you can help me Karl-Heinz. Do you see my wardrobe over there?' Karl-Heinz nodded.

'You find me a dressing gown and help me to put it on, will you?'

We sat around her kitchen table having the lunch I had brought when Frau Bucker asked: 'When are you going to tell me what's happened whilst I was away? Nobody would give me any information at the hospital, although I kept asking and I know you were not supposed to worry me during your visits. I am at home now and really need to know.' She looked straight into my eyes whilst she said it.

'As far as I know the battles in France are still continuing. The German Armies have suffered heavy casualties, one of them being the Field Marshal.'

'The Field Marshal? Is he.... ? 'No', I interrupted. 'He survived but is badly wounded. Mind you, every bit of information we get is giving us a different version, so you do not know whom or what to believe.

161

According to the German Authorities, he is in an army hospital near his home town. We pray they are telling us the truth. We have heard nothing about it from the BBC.

'How did it happen?' Frau Bucker asked.

'I heard that his car was hit by an attacking British Aircraft.'

'Hilde, that is terrible news, let's hope he will be alright. Oh, no, where is Karl?' she now asked.

'I don't know, I haven't heard anything. I went over to the old garrison to see whether anybody there knew, but they are also in the dark, just as we are.'

A loud banging on her front door stopped us in our tracks.

'Frau Bucker, is Hilde with you?' It was Maria. We let her in. Maria was panting.

'Erika phoned, I raced to get here.'

'What happened? Is she alright? Does she want me to phone her back?' I went to get my bag ready to go.

'No, no, wait, let me get my breath.' Maria was still panting heavily. The recent diet of starchy food, without any nutrients had not helped her already heavy figure. Every time we went anywhere together she seemed to be gasping for air after a short walk. I had been worried about it for a while now, especially after what had happened to Frau Bucker .

'Erika specifically said you cannot phone her back. They are packing everything up at the Communication Centre. She is leaving for Tilsit later today.'

'What? I have to go and phone her, something must have happened.' I was getting frantic now.

'There has been an assassination attempt on the Fuehrer's life.'

Stunned silence.

Frau Bucker then said, 'An assassination attempt, what does that mean?'

'Erika said there is a lot of confusion, but he survived.'

'Failed! The attempt failed, that's what it means.' The two looked at me after my outburst.

'Where was this attempt, did she know?'

'East Prussia.'

'East Prussia? Oh my God!' Karl where are you? Went through my mind instantly.

Chapter 54

'What was that?' Maria asked. We had just collected Klaus, Hugo and Renate from school. On Saturdays the schools finished early and we were waiting by the gate at about 12.30. Because it was a short day at school the children would not get a meal there and as a treat we promised them we would to go to *Cero*, which was everybody's favourite Ice Cream parlour.

It was not very far from the school, just about a 15 minute walk. We had to pass the theatre before we got there, and it still excited me every time I saw it, thinking back to the time when theatre was part of my Life.

I looked at Klaus, who was so tall now. It was the end of July 1944 and he was already seven years old.

Hannelore said she would meet us at *Cero*. She had started to work in the town at the large Department Store and would spend her lunchtime with us.

'Where are Frau Bucker and Inge?' she asked when she joined us at our table by the window.

'It was a little bit too far for Frau Bucker to walk. She said she will make up for it when all her strength has returned. Inge is working today.'

'Today? I thought she has every second Saturday off?' Hannelore said.

'She has, but she wanted a free day next week for her mother's birthday and they agreed she could do that if she worked today.' I said

'What was that?' Maria asked again.

'That sounded like a bomb!' Hannelore shouted and jumped up to look out of the window.

Then more loud bangs, in short succession. Now everybody in the Ice Cream parlour was on their feet, some pushing their chairs

163

over trying to get to the front door. Mothers with children, who were protesting because the ice cream had just arrived.

The owner now shouted, 'The theatre, everybody get to the theatre, the cellars there are used as the nearest bomb shelter.'

Hannelore grabbed Karl-Heinz and Manfred. I put Ursula back into her pushchair and she wailed with being handled so roughly. 'Klaus, take Renate's and Hugo's hand. NOW!' I shouted.

'But, Mamma, I haven't finished my ice cream.' It was so unlike Klaus to cry but the tears were rolling down his face.

I just took him by the arm and pushed the children out of the door. 'Come on.' I tried to keep calm but to no avail.

We got there as fast as we could. The theatre was only about 150 meters away. I did not want to lose sight of the children and kept calling their names whilst we continued. Maria was behind me. I had no time to turn around but I could hear Maria panting. There must have been over 200 people running in the same direction. All the time the loud noises in the distance continued.

I could see smoke rising to the West..

The theatre cellar had a familiar smell. All theatres must smell the same, I thought. We found a place between old costumes and sat on the floor. Karl-Heinz had his hands over his ears and his eyes closed. Ursula wanted to run around and was fighting my attempt to hold her close.

Renate said, 'Mamma, I need the toilet.'

'Me too,' said Karl-Heinz, who saw it as an opportunity to leave the dark room.

I got up to see where I could take them, to the delight of Ursula, who had escaped my grasp and toddled off. Hannelore got to her just in time, gave her back to me and said: 'I will take Renate and Karl-Heinz.'

'Please be careful Hannelore and hurry.' I did not like the three of them going somewhere without me.

'Could you see in which directions the bombs fell?' Maria now asked.

'I saw smoke to the West,' I replied.

The theatre warden arrived. 'Listen, we got the 'all clear', you can all go home now.'

164

Everybody stumbled back onto their feet and surrounded the warden asking questions.

'Was there a bomb attack? Where did they drop? Is anybody injured? I did not hear any warning sirens? Did you hear the 'all clear' yourself?' Everybody shouted at the same time.

'People, please!' the warden tried to guide us toward the exit. 'Yes I have heard the all clear, but I have no information, please go to your homes. Maybe there will be some announcements later.'

Hannelore was already outside. 'I had better get back to the store, maybe it is closed now but I still have to go. There are instructions issued by the store owner and I have to follow them.'

Frau Bucker was looking out of her kitchen window waiting for us. She was outside my apartment door before we entered the building.

'Oh, thank God! Thank God you are alright! What happened?'

'We don't know, but the smoke is coming from the West. Did you hear any warning sirens?' I replied.

'No, nothing, but I did hear the 'all clear'. We all hid downstairs when we heard the bombs. 'Where is Hannelore?' she now asked.

'She went back to the store, she will be home soon. Klaus, go upstairs to see Hannelore's Grandmother and tell her she is fine and she should be back home shortly.'

'Can I go?' asked Hugo. 'Me too,' said Renate and Karl-Heinz. They all knew that sometimes Hannelore's Grandmother had some biscuits and with good news like this, there was a chance they would all get one.

Before the children came back downstairs, I saw a boy from the kitchen window, running down the street. He came to our entrance and seconds after that, started banging on my door.

'Frau Paekel! Frau Paekel! Are you there, Frau Paekel?'

Maria was the nearest to the door and opened it. It was Inge's younger brother.

'Frau Paekel, please come, my mother said to fetch you. Please come.' He was now in the kitchen, rushed over and pulled me by my arm. 'Please come.'

'Friedhelm, yes of course but what has happened, is it your mother?' I asked looking at him. He looked in a right state. His face was dirty, where he had dried his tears with his hands. He had no shoes on, like he had just run off to get me without a second thought.

'It's Inge,' he managed to get out. 'They've bombed the sugar factory!'

Chapter 55

Smoke, burning fires, and lots of smoke. We could not get very close to the bomb site. Noises, loud noises, screams, shouts, fire sirens. People, lots and lots of people. We were pushed back. Further back, away from the site.

'Inge! Inge!' If it was not Inge's mother calling her name, it was Inge's brother or me. 'Inge! Inge!' over and over again.

Earlier when I got to where Inge lived with her family, her mother was already outside the door.

'Hilde, I have got to get to the Sugar Factory. Inge! I have to find Inge!' She kept wiping her hands on the floral-printed overall she was wearing whilst cooking. I recognised the pattern, a mauve flowery print. Inge had bought it at Christmas and I had helped her wrap it up. Inge's mother's hands were completely dry, but she kept wiping them.

I saw the desperation etched on her face. I stepped into the road and stood in front of the first car coming along. The driver stopped, only just avoiding me, opened the door and started to shout. Before I could work out what he actually said, I opened the passenger door and said, 'We have to get to the sugar factory.' The driver just stared at me. I pulled Inge's mother over. 'Her daughter works there and the factory has just been bombed.'

'Get in.'

It took far too long to get there, or so we thought. The roads were blocked, with emergency vehicles, military lorries, cars, peoples on motorcycles, pushbikes or running and walking.

When the car got near to the factory we got out and ran along with everybody else.

By now wardens had taken over command, directing the fire engines and shouting instructions to groups of people digging with their bare hands trying to shift the still smouldering rubble.

'My daughter, have you seen my daughter?' Inge's mother asked the nearest warden.

'Does she work here?' he inquired.

'Yes, today is her day off but she came in today. You see, it is my birthday next week and she wanted to spend it with me, so she worked today instead. Have you seen her?' She pulled on his arm.

'Are you three together?' he now addressed me.

I nodded, he would have not heard a reply over the noise.' Go over there and give your details to the soldier in charge, he is gathering all the information, getting the names of the people who worked here today. He also has the names of the people already accounted for.'

Inge's mother had already gone in the direction the warden had pointed. 'Inge! Inge!'

Inge was not with the others. We eventually found somebody who worked with her, a young man about Inge's age.

'Inge went to get some coffee the last time I saw her, that was shortly before the first bomb fell,' he told us.

The soldier co-ordinating the rescue overheard him and asked 'Where would that be in relation to your office?'

'The canteen is at the other end of the building, over there. Do you see the fire over there? That is where it should be.'

He realised what he had just said, put his hands over his mouth, looked at Inge's mother and exclaimed, 'Oh my God. Oh no!'

'Give me your daughter's name and I'll go and get the list,' said the soldier now.

'What list?'

'Some people have been taken to the hospital and then there are others still missing. We need you to give us all the information so we can to find out what happened to your daughter.'

'Young man,' he now addressed Inge's colleague, 'you come along as well, maybe you can go over the list with us to see whether it is complete.'

Inge's name was not on the list of people taken to the hospital. Inge's name had not been added at all. Officially she was not working today, so nobody had thought of reporting her missing.

168

'How many other people could there be who have not been reported so far?' The soldier asked the young man with whom Inge worked.

'I, I don't know' he stammered, now feeling guilty that he had not thought of checking where Inge was, or reporting her missing.

The lookouts on the tower, to raise the alarm in case of an imminent air attack, had been withdrawn three days before the bombing of the Sugar Factory. The soldiers were needed elsewhere. The town had arranged for sirens to be placed on some of the shops instead, but these were not operational on that day.

Every day one of us went with Inge's mother to the bomb site. More bodies were discovered daily but nobody had yet reached the canteen. We knew that shouting out for Inge had become pointless, but it gave her mother some comfort that perhaps her daughter could hear us and knew we were there.

Inge's mother never gave up hope. It took two weeks to find all the bodies, some of them were unidentifiable. Where the canteen had been, after the rubble had been removed, they found eight people, lying on top of each other. To spare Inge's mother further pain, Maria and I accompanied Inge's brother to try and identify and hopefully claim her body.

The same soldier who had organised the initial search, shook his head when we arrived.

He turned to Inge's brother. 'I am so sorry, young man, we cannot be sure, which one is your sister.'

'We have got to find Inge,' he said to Maria and me and we agreed we would all go to check on the unidentified remains.

The stench was overwhelming but we never flinched. Inge deserved better than us turning away from her.

The soldier went to the back of the lorry and uncovered the last two bodies. One was obviously male judging by the size. The other one was curled up and round her neck clearly visible was a silver necklace. The roses on the necklace had not melted from the extreme heat that the fire must have generated.

'Inge,' we sobbed, Inge was still wearing the necklace I had given her long ago one Christmas Eve.

169

The night before Inge's funeral the sirens went off and we cowered in the dark in the cellar of our apartment block until the all clear was given.

There was a big turnout to lay Inge to rest. Her remaining colleagues from work, thirty four of them had perished that day. Inge's family and friends, all of us, everybody from my apartment block, storekeepers and their families from our nearby shops. We all wept openly in the little Chapel at the *Lamberty Cemetery*. We walked behind her coffin and saw it being lowered into the ground. We had managed to get some roses and one by one our children stepped forward to let their rose follow her into the earth and said their final farewell.

Chapter 56

14th October 1944
Hildesheim

The feeling of death all around us would not leave me. Field Marshal Rommel was dead. The radio announcement was repeated late at night, finishing again with a military band playing the funeral march. Gone was any hope which we might have had. For the children's sake, we managed to struggle through the days which followed.

Field Marshal Rommel's State funeral was going to be held on October the 18th 1944 in Ulm. We wanted to go and see the newsreel at the picture house the following week. We had not been there for a long time and had no intention of seeing the full programme. We would leave after the weekly news, which we hoped would cover the Field Marshal's funeral. It did, but only for a few minutes. As soon as Field Marshal Rommel's final procession had left, it switched back to its usual propaganda, just like nothing had happened. We got up and left.

I spent each day in a trance. I could not think of anything else. It seemed like life was fading away. I knew that as long as Field Marshal Rommel was looking after his troops, they would be alright.

And then he was home. Two weeks after the Field Marshal's funeral, Karl walked down the road towards our apartment. I spotted him through the kitchen window, where I had spent a lot of time lately. He was coming round the corner and I shouted, 'Klaus! Renate! Karl-Heinz! Your Pappa is home! Quick, you run and get him!'

'Me go,' said Ursula. 'No, you stay with Mamma, you will fall.' I told her but she kept trying to pull away. Once we were on the pavement I let her go as well.

Although Karl looked happy being surrounded by his children I could sense a deep sadness within in.

'Just hold me, Fraulein Hilde,' he said when it was my turn to greet him. The children around him were all talking at once. Karl picked up Ursula and carried her back in. 'Pappa home,' she said.

'Why, Karl, why could the doctors not save the Field Marshal?' I asked him later.

'I saw him three weeks ago and he was fit and well.'

'What do you mean he was fit and well?' I looked at Karl who seemed to struggle with himself to answer.

'He was well and made new plans.'

'What are you saying Karl?'

'Some of us don't think that he died of his injuries.'

Chapter 57

In December of 1944, I received a letter from my sister Erika.
'*My dear Sister,*
I cannot begin to tell you how life up here has changed. Our mother is a shadow of her former self. When I speak to her, I think she does not hear me or pretends not to. I think her whole world has collapsed around her.

We have never heard a word from Arno since he left, which must be by now over six years ago. Both Herbert and Helmut are somewhere fighting a War. Gisela is working and doing her best to help at home. Traute, not yet fifteen years old, has gone. She likes the good life and has moved in with a Russian officer. Our mother went to the police to report it, but you can imagine what they said. We should be happy that the Russians have not yet burned our house down, or words to that effect.

Lisbet has long departed, went back to her former husband who lives in a small place in Saxony 'Limbach-Oberfrona'.

And only last week Guenter was drafted. Who knows where they have sent him? A boy of fourteen.

Thank God for sending us Oleg, Ludmilla and their children. If it were not for them, I think our mother would have killed herself by now. They keep everything together and work our land. Oleg is very resourceful and cunning. He is a master in dealing and bargaining. Plus he speaks good enough Russian for the Russian Authorities to have some kind of respect.

There has been a bomb attack on Konigsberg last month and the town burned for several days. Now the Russian Armies have marched in. Many people have fled towards Berlin and others are planning to follow. There is a fear here that the Russian Armies will take total control soon. There would be nobody left to tell the tale when they take over completely.

I am glad I came back when I did. Secretly, Oleg, Ludmilla, Gisela and I are planning our escape. Gisela has a boyfriend now, he is also in the Army of course. She met him at work one day when he wanted to buy some fabrics to take back to his mother on a home visit. His mother lives in 'Sondershausen' which is east of the Harz Mountains. That is where she wants to go to of course.

Mother knows nothing of our plan. When we work out which route we will take and when we feel safe to do so, we will just pack her few belongings and drag her along. I hope she will not protest. Meanwhile, we are preparing and storing things in our old hiding place. Oleg still has his small truck and we hope it will last. Everybody in our family has your address for keeping in touch and as a possible meeting point. I hope you don't mind.

I cannot phone you anymore, I do not have an office to go to and I will not risk speaking openly from a phone booth.

I hope this letter reaches you, I am giving it to a friend who will forward it hopefully from Berlin.

I hope I will see you soon, I miss you so much.

With Love your Sister Erika

PS. Don't worry about me, I am fine

PPS. Told Erich not to come on leave here. He might be in touch with you instead.

I put Erika's letter down after I had read it a few times. It had no dates on it, so I did not know when she wrote it, but the postmark from Berlin had a stamp on it 15th November 1944. That was just over one month ago.

'Don't worry about me, she says!' I told Karl when I passed the letter over. 'She has no idea how worried I am.' 'When do you think she wrote it?' I asked.

'We heard about Konigsberg burning, that was about the beginning of October. Let's see, Erika refers to it as 'last month' so I think she wrote the letter not long before it was posted. That means beginning of November.' Karl said.

'I wonder whether they have left by now? I will write to Helene in Berlin, she might know something. Maybe that is where they are planning to go to.'

'Be careful what you say in your letter,' Karl reminded me.

'I will, I'll just ask her whether she has heard anything from home.'

'Do you think you will soon be posted somewhere?'

'I have not received any instructions, and I hope they will just leave me here. Karl looked frightened when he faced me and continued, 'Although I doubt it very much.'

Chapter 58

Karl's deployment arrived on a snowy night at the beginning of February 1945.

It was delivered by hand. The dreaded knock on the door. Something we knew would happen but feared nevertheless. The banging was so loud and relentless it woke most of our neighbours. Some were already awake from the noise of the jeeps and the heavy boots of the Gestapo.

Karl jumped out of bed to reach the door as fast as he could in the hope that the children would not have to witness what was facing him.

It was too late for that, all four got up and stood at our bedside. Renate was holding Ursula's hand. Our children did not make a sound, thinking it was another alarm, which meant they had to be very quiet, get ready in the dark and make their way into the cellar. Klaus had already gone back into their room, to get some clothes and blankets.

'Officer Paekel?' the first Gestapo man asked.

I could see our neighbours on the staircase and Frau Bucker appeared pushing her way through to come into our apartment.

'Yes,' Karl replied.

'Your new deployment has just come through, we were instructed to hand it to you immediately,' the Gestapo man smirked.

I now noticed it was our old postman, who had told me years ago that the future was with the Nazi Party. Some future that was.

'Don't you want to know where you are being drafted to?' He was curious to see our reaction when we found out.

But I did not want to give him that satisfaction. I was now at the door and said, 'Yes, but we can read!' and slammed the door closed, almost hitting his face. Inwardly I shook like a leaf. I did not feel brave at all.

'Come on, children. There is no bombing tonight, let's put you back into bed.' With that Frau Bucker shepherded the children out of the hall and into their room. Later I heard the front door closing quietly behind her when she went back up to her own place.

'Karl, talk to me, what does it say?' His hands were shaking so much, he could not keep hold of the paper and it slowly fell onto the floor.

'The Russian Front, I expected as much!' Karl said.

'The Russian Front? Why Karl? The Russians have already entered Poland and Prussia. Why are you being sent to the Russian Front?' I was frantic now. I bent down to retrieve it, maybe he had misread it but I knew it was true, I just did not want it to be.

Karl just stared at the letter now in my hand .

'What if you just don't go? Just stay here with us. What would they do?'

'You know that Gestapo postman you just saw invading our home? He would not think twice about it and without hesitation would pull the trigger and would shoot me in front of our children, with the same grin on his face as he had, giving me this notice. Is that what we want, Hilde?'

'Karl, please don't go. Maybe in the morning you can go to your old Garrison, they may be able to stop your deployment, or at least get an extension. Please at least try it.'

'There is no point. I am an officer, I will have to follow orders, I will have to go.'

'How much time have we got?'

'Until tomorrow,' he looked at our clock which stood on top of our sitting room cupboard showing it to be past midnight. 'No, today, early afternoon. I have to take a train about 14.00 hours.'

Chaos greeted us at the train station. People shoving and pushing. Mothers with little children in pushchairs, with one hand hanging on to their young sons in uniform; old women with their husbands looking confused. Why would their husbands have to go to war at their age? Some of the older men were not able to stand up straight, their backs stooped and they only just managed to shuffle along. All the time being pushed forward with instructions by the Gestapo. Steam and noises from the trains, which seemed like wild

177

animals straining to go. I was holding on to Karl as tight as I could trying to keep up with him, moving along outside the train trying to spot a free place inside.

A woman in a heavy fur coat, a scarf around her had stepped out in front of us.

'You!' she pointed to Karl. 'Please take him with you and look after him. Keep him safe for me.' With that she pulled her young son into view. The uniform was swamping his small frame, his field cap pulled over his ears. The rucksack on his back made him arch backwards and he was holding his helmet in one hand. He could not have been more than thirteen years old. She did not wait for Karl's answer but instead faced her son and said, 'Paul, you go with him, you hear? He looks kind. Do not leave his side.' She hugged him and was gone.

Karl now looked at the terrified boy in front of him, took him by his shoulder and told him, 'Well, Paul, I believe it is you and me now, your first task is to find us both a seat.'

'Yes, Sir.' You could hear the relief in his voice when he went through the open train door and vanished inside. He appeared a few minutes later.

'Sir, I have two seats for us in the next carriage. I have put my rucksack there already. Shall I go ahead?'

'Yes, Paul, I will be there shortly.'

The train whistle blew, which was the sign to hurry up. A Gestapo man came over. 'You have to board the train now, you don't want it to leave without you, do you?'

'Yes, Karl, please let it go without you. You just missed the train, what can they do? I would not let go of his coat.

Karl turned to face me, his face a deathly grey. My legs were shaking and I was in danger of collapsing, it was only my tight grip on his coat which kept me upright.

'Hilde, it is time for us to say goodbye.' He had to prise my .fingers off his sleeve one by one. The impatient whistling of the train blew angry steam in our direction. It should have been hot, but all I felt was an icy blast. Karl pulled me towards him held me for a few seconds, kissed me and said, 'I love you, Fraulein Hilde, don't you ever forget it.'

Already on the steps he turned round. His eyes never leaving mine. He still stood there although the train had started to move.

I started running alongside. 'Karl, Karl, I will hold you to your promise.'

'Which promise?' I heard him shouting back.

'You promised to take me to Italy to visit the Monastery in Monte Cassino.' The train had gathered speed and I was not sure whether he had heard me.

'Karl! Karl!' I was still shouting his name, although the train had disappeared in a cloud of smoke.

Chapter 59

22nd of March 1945
Hildesheim, Germany

'Run! Run! Faster! Faster!' I was the first one to hear it, a rumbling behind us. I looked round and then up. The sky, which a moment ago was blue and bright, was now dark and threatening, like a flock of angry birds looking for their prey.

The noise was deafening. There, again and again, getting closer and closer.

We grabbed the hands of our children. Maria pulled the pushchair with her right hand and held Manfred with her left. He stumbled and fell to the ground. She lifted him back up and half running, half being dragged along, they carried on. Nobody made a sound.

I had a tight grip on Karl-Heinz and Ursula on my arm Her weight slowed me down but I did not feel the ache in my muscles or the pain from the scratches on my body. The undergrowth was dense, the brambles tore at our dresses. There was a noise right in front of us, we froze. A young deer stopped in its tracks, looked at us and sped away.

A whistle sound, just like one of those fireworks at New Year's Eve, right overhead. Followed by a split second of silence. Total silence. Then an ear-splitting sound and the earth moved around us.

'Down! Get down!' We all fell to the ground; I shielded Ursula and Karl-Heinz with my body and covered my head with my arms. It was like a hailstorm: a debris of stones, splintered wood and soil were hitting our bodies.

'Hilde, are you alright?' Maria was up first, brushing dirt off her clothes.

'We have to leave the pushchair. Hurry! Hurry!'

We kept on running, ducking in and out of trees, the moss soft under our feet. I looked around to take a deep breath and to make sure that we were alone when we got there.

I knew this place so well. We would be safe there for a while.

The door, although it was old and the hinges were rusty, was strong. There was a big iron ring on one of the sides, you have to pull hard and hold it with both hands to lift it up.

'Quick! Quick! In here!' I ushered everybody down the stairs, took a large stone, which was lying in the shadows and I used it to keep the trapdoor slightly open. I could not know how long we might be in here and we needed the air. We crouched down and huddled together, the floor in our hiding place shook, the walls vibrated and dust was sprinkling down on us. We had reached the tower just in time.

How could I have been so foolish, taking this risk and endangering all our lives?

It had been such a beautiful day, the first warm day of Spring. I had taken the children over to Maria, the short walk to the end of the road. Ursula wanted to walk and together, with Karl-Heinz, Ursula held on to her pushchair.

'Come on, Maria, we will be alright, we have not taken the children out for such a long time.'

She was not convinced, but finally was persuaded, relented and gave in. 'As far as the tower, and no further,' she had argued.

'Mamma, I am scared.' 'Shush, Karl-Heinz, come over here.' I had to whisper, no need to frighten the others.

I pulled him up on my lap and held him close. I gently stroked his face and hummed to him quietly. Ursula clung to me, her tiny arms firmly round my neck, not wanting to let go.

We took comfort by sitting closely together. It was dark down there but we were starting to adjust. The light, which was coming from upstairs through the gap I left, was unusually dim for this time of the day. It should only be around 2 pm in the afternoon. Why did it look so dark?

I smelled smoke, which seemed to be creeping down through the space at the top and was now rolling down the stairs to get at us.

Then another whistle sound, silence and an almighty blast. We fell backwards from the impact. I could make out a rattle from the door above me, dropped Karl-Heinz on the floor and raced upstairs. I reached the door just before the stone rolled away. I used my back to lift it up with all the strength left inside me.

'Maria, take the children, I am going to have a look.'

She stared at me. 'But we have not heard the all clear.'

I stopped in my tracks, why did we not hear the warnings from sirens placed throughout the town?

'Seventy-five, seventy-six, seventy-seven.' The stones steps are steep and slightly damp and I had never climbed them this fast. There were only 20 steps to go. These were on the round iron staircase which was narrow and could be slippery at times. It was best to hold on to the rail. The paint was flaking off, leaving sharp edges cutting my hand as I continued upstairs. Reaching the top I wiped my hands on my dress, leaving dark smudges.

I knew the tower was deserted now and it was quite safe to come here again.

Just in case, I crouched down, slowly lifting my head above the last step and looked around before I stood up.

It was hazy and a little lighter up here but the smell of smoke made me choke. I lifted my dress to cover my nose whilst trying to feel my way towards the front of the tower, edging forward very slowly. The last time I was here I saw that part of the walls were crumbling and some of the stones had fallen down to the ground below.

What seemed like a long way, shuffling forward, one foot at the time, I reached the front. Through the smoke I could make out fires in the distance but I could not see clearly and there was nothing I could do from here. We had to get back.

I carried Ursula on my hip, held Karl-Heinz with a firm grip with my right hand, Maria and Manfred were behind me. We made our way to the end of the forest. The journey back was blocked by fallen trees, smouldering rubble and there were fires burning to our left. It was easier for me to climb over the trees, so I went first. Maria lifted the children over one by one and then I helped Maria. After the third climb we were getting into a routine and managed to go faster. We reached the end of the woods, where we stopped dead trying to take in what we saw.

Waterloo Strasse, which should have been in front of us, had disappeared. Where there once were houses, there were now smouldering ruins. Fires were burning everywhere. People were shouting, running, trying to save their homes by forming lines passing buckets of water to each other. Children were wandering aimlessly, lost, crying, looking bewildered, some sitting on remains of walls, which a short while ago had been their home.

The way back was like running the gauntlet: we weaved through the chaos around us, fell over but got up and continued on. We passed bodies in the streets, people searching to identify members of their families, calling out names of loved ones. We tried to shield the children from what we witnessed. Maria took Ursula for a while. Our hands held onto our children very tightly, children who had lost the will to walk.

We saw some of the furniture on the pavement, long before we got to my apartment. Frau Bucker spotted us and came running, shouting all the way. 'Hilde! Hilde! Come! Come!' I could not understand immediately what she was trying to tell me, most of it was lost in the noise and her voice seemed to be doing somersaults. From the distance I could see the roof had been hit and flames were shooting up into the sky.

'Hilde! The school! Leave everything and get to the school!' All blood drained from me as she said it. Our children! We had sent the elder children to school in the morning .I looked down at my feet, my stockings were torn, bloody scratches across my legs, a heel on one of my shoes was missing. I snapped off the other heel, looked at Maria and ran.

Chapter 60

I ran. Frau Bucker's words ringing in my ears. 'Hilde! The school! Leave everything and get to the school!' But how? Everywhere there were blazing fires and the streets blocked with smouldering debris. People shouting. Again passing buckets of water from one person to another in the futile attempt to save a few belongings. Other mothers running in the same direction as me. The children from our part of the town all went to the same school. Two women sped towards me and I stopped. I recognised one of them, the mother of Renate's school friend. The girl she met on her first day at school.

We had to shout to each other trying to be heard over the noises around us.

'Do you know whether the school was hit?' I asked.

'We don't know, we have seen people running in the direction of the school but most of them came back. There is a big crater at the end of the road. We have to find another way. We turned around. 'Let's go via the railway station, it's longer but there is less smoke on that side of the town,' suggested one of the mothers.

They looked at me and saw the state I was in, bleeding from the run through the woods, torn clothes, shoes without heels, and my pregnancy was beginning to show.

'Can you manage?' they asked.

I nodded. I would get to our children no matter what.

The damage was just as great on the route we were now trying to take, but this way the fires were now being put out using fire engines. The Fire Brigade had tried to open a corridor for people to get through.

We stopped to catch our breath for only a few seconds. I bent over because I thought I was going to be sick from the stench. One of the mothers put her arm around my waist and stopped me from falling. I stood back up ready to carry on but the sight of the devastation in front of us was paralysing my whole body. Our town, *Hildesheim*, had disappeared. As far as I could see there was only rubble, some burning out of control and some smouldering away. By now I guessed it was about two hours since we were hiding at the tower and people here were already starting a clean-up and rescue mission.

We found a way through to the school and I immediately felt better. The school was damaged but was not burning. Teachers were directing children to different areas of the playground. The children waited patiently in line according to their classes.

Renate saw me. 'Mamma, I am here.' I raced over to where she was and wrapped my arms around her. Klaus and Hugo had seen me too and came running towards us.

'Mamma, Mamma.'

'Aunty Hilde, where is my Mamma?' Hugo asked me.

'Your Mamma is looking after Manfred, Karl-Heinz and Ursula. She is waiting for us at home. They are fine.'

'Mamma, did anybody die?' Klaus asked.

Before I could reply one of the teachers carrying a list of names came over. 'Frau Paekel, are you taking Hugo with you?' Hugo immediately took hold of my hand. 'I can cross his name off the list 'Children Awaiting Collection' then' she continued.

'Are all the children and teachers alright?'

'Most of them are accounted for', she said. Some have been hurt, and a couple of teachers are still missing.'

'Mamma, we had to run into the cellar when the planes came. I was just playing outside with my friends,' Renate said. 'Mamma, we had to wear our gas masks. Look,' she said and pulled it over her face.

'It was lucky that the children had just had their lunch break and everybody was outside, otherwise we would not have seen the planes coming,' the teacher told us.

'Mamma, can we go home now?' asked Klaus.

Maria's apartment block was severely damaged. It was too dangerous to stay there. Frau Bucker had an old cart in her part of

185

the communal cellar. We pulled it over to Maria's home and loaded it up with everything we would need, especially whatever was left in kitchen cupboards. She secured her home as best as she could. We pulled a full cart back to my place.

The roof of our apartment block had burned out but the fire hadn't spread. Most of Hannelore's and her grandparent's belongings were gone, but at least they were safe. Hannelore and her family moved in with Frau Bucker. Maria and her children moved in with me. Together we all shared what few things we still had and tried to survive.

Chapter 61

A matter of survival, day by day, that's what is was. We learned that half the population of our town had been bombed out and many people had nowhere to go. Others did not want to leave the place where their home had been. For the first few nights after the bombing the elderly, mainly women, just sat silently outside their former homes in shock.

We tried to help us much as we could. Maria was an excellent organizer. The first thing she did was go around our neighbourhood collecting addresses of houses still or partly intact and checked whether anybody had room for one or two extra persons. The spirit of the people was amazing. Within the first few days we had found accommodation for over thirty people.

Inge's mother found extra space for another two; Frau Bucker took in an elderly woman, a friend of Hannelore's Grandmother. Our other neighbours helped several more. By now our street had become a community of about one hundred and other areas followed Maria's example.

People who had never met before started to help each other and gave whatever anybody could spare. Maria, myself and several young boys went out to survey the damage in the town, to see whether the Town Hall was operational, whether there was any information where and how to get any food, or whether we now needed any coupons. We also checked with our important contacts, the black markets. In the evenings we shared what we had learned with others and they in turn informed us what they knew. The local Garrison was almost intact and we convinced the few soldiers still there that we should make it our meeting point. Also for collection and distribution of clothing and blankets and most important, set up a soup kitchen. In storage there were some field rations which we begged them for and used those until we managed to find other sources. Nobody took any notice of the SS or the Gestapo. It was as if our fears had disappeared with the destruction of our town.

'Do you think there will be another air raid?' one elderly woman asked us a few days after the attack, whilst collecting some food rations from the Garrison.

The young soldier packing up a carton for her answered: 'What is there still to bomb?'

Klaus and Hugo now helped at the Garrison, it was only at the corner of our road so we let them go. Our other children stayed with Frau Bucker. She and Hannelore, together with some elderly women, had taken over looking after all the children now living in our apartment block, so most of us could do other tasks. Some stronger younger women and boys took the carts to farmers. They took whatever valuables we still had in order to bargain for potatoes, vegetables, chickens, flour, whatever we could get. I parted with my gold watch Maria had given me on Christmas Eve, the same Christmas Eve I had given Inge her necklace.

Maria spotted me handing it over and took it back.

'But, Maria!' I protested.

'I understand, really I do, but we might need it some other time.' She took off a heavy solid silver bracelet and gave it to the woman who was going with the group pushing the cart to a village about 10 kilometres away, with the instruction to only hand it over for some meat. The rest of us then started our daily work of clearing the rubble trying to regain some sort of order.

After a few weeks this had become our now normal way of life.

In the evenings when our children were asleep, Frau Bucker and Hannelore would join us and we would sit around the radio in my sitting room listening to German and British broadcasts. We heard about other towns being bombed. From the British Broadcast we learned that the British Troops had liberated a concentration camp at Bergen Belsen. This was only about 60 km from here. How could there be such a camp holding thousands of women and children so close to where we lived without our knowledge?

'What is a concentration camp?' asked Hannelore.

188

Frau Bucker was the first to speak. 'We have heard whispers for a while now, Hannelore,' she said. 'People, mainly Jewish, are picked up in the middle of the night and sent to labour camps. Our Jewish community here was very small and most of them left after the burning of the Synagogue or shortly after. You are too young to remember that night.'

'But I know some Jewish people, they are still here, are they in danger of being taken away?' Hannelore now asked.

'No, I know who you mean and they are safe enough. They either have a non-Jewish husband or wife.'

Now we had learned that the British Army was in such close proximity to where we lived we made sure we would tune to both stations each night. The British Broadcast and the 'Reichssender Hamburg' were the only German stations still on air.

1st May 1945, at 22.30 hours. We sat around the radio when the announcement came.

'Reports from the Fuehrer's Headquarters, Hitler has fallen at his command post in the Reich's Chancery, fighting to the last breath against Bolshevism and for Germany. Hitler previously appointed Grand Admiral Doenitz as his successor. Now follows an announcement by Admiral Doenitz.'

'German People, I call upon you to mourn your Fuehrer, who died the death of a hero.'

Total silence in my sitting room for several minutes, then:

'What does that mean?' Hannelore wanted to know.

'That means we thank God the day has finally come,' said Frau Bucker

Chapter 62

8th of May 1945, the signing by Germany of the Act of Unconditional Surrender at a schoolhouse in Reims in North East France was announced today. It was signed by General Jodl for Germany, General Bedell-Smith for Britain and her Allies, General Francois Sevez for France and Ivan Susloparov for Russia.

The British Prime Minister, Winston Churchill, spoke from his office in 10 Downing Street proclaiming victory and the end of the War in Europe.

We were waiting for this broadcast all day, not venturing outside. Hildesheim had already been taken over by British and American Forces over a week ago. From the reaction of the soldiers when they arrived in convoys, we realised how shocked they were at what they found. That the town they were supposed to be assigned to was reduced to rubble.

The first thing they did was to set up tents near the airfield about two or three kilometres north of our street. When the wind came from the North, we could smell the cooking from the camp. More and more people, mainly young women and boys, started to wait outside their camp in the hope of a hot meal or the odd piece of chocolate.

With the arrival of the British and American Armies came the disappearance of the SS and Gestapo men. Not one of them was anywhere to be seen. It was like the earth had swallowed them up.

'I have heard that most of them are burning their uniforms at night in the cellars of bombed-out buildings. If they spot anybody coming to check what the fires are about, they scatter or claim ignorance. If questioned they deny ever having belonged to the party,' Frau Bucker told me when we sat in the kitchen , peeling potatoes and cleaning vegetables for the soup we were making. Enough for about twenty people to eat.

We never knew that we had a Prisoner of War camp, but there had in fact been one nearby. Apparently it had been hit during the second bombing raid during 1944 and some of the Allied Prisoners of War had been killed. These were the first buildings to be requisitioned by the British troops. After that they took over most of the Garrisons. The Garrisons which until now had housed some of the general population who had lost their homes and were now forced to move again into overcrowded schools, the cinema, theatre or any houses which were judged to be big enough to accommodate more people. Some people moved out altogether in the faint hope of finding accommodation in nearby villages.

Our Garrison, at the end of the street, was now British but we were allowed to keep a small partitioned-off corner and continue our efforts, with food collection, distribution and the soup kitchen.

'You have been looking out of the window for a long time now, Hilde. What are you looking for?' Frau Bucker asked.

I turned around to face her, wiping my wet hands on a tea towel. 'Karl, I am hoping to spot Karl when he comes round the corner. I want it to be me, the first person he sees when he returns. The War is over. Karl can come home now and we can be a complete family at last.'

Chapter 63

October 1945
Hildesheim

'Karl! Karl !' I was shouting his name. I spotted more returning soldiers coming down the street. They always had to pass my kitchen window on the way to the Garrison to report in, giving their details and handing over any weapons which they might still have.

I had no time to check on my new baby but grabbed Ursula by the arm, pulling her all the way and ran outside towards the soldiers before they would pass our apartment block. I was in my slippers and without a coat. Ursula was still in her pink pyjamas.

This time there must have been about thirty of them. 'Karl! Karl?' A wounded soldier, his head heavily bandaged, one leg shorter than the other, he supported himself on some wooden crutches. I looked into his face for a sign of recognition, he raised his head which until now had been bent down towards the floor, looked at me and shook it.

'Do you know my Karl?' I asked another.

'Where do you come from?' I asked the next. 'Are you all from the same Brigade?'

'Do you know whether there are more soldiers on the way?' I asked the same questions day in and day out. Always being greeted with the same sad looks.

'Karl! Karl,' maybe he was at the back of the group.

Frau Bucker came to find me and took Ursula and carried her back. I now saw Ursula was in her bare feet.

Maria, who was by now living back in her old apartment, had seen the soldiers returning before they entered the street where I lived and was by my side before Frau Bucker had reached me. Maria and Frau Bucker looked at each other.

'Karl! Karl! I would not stop shouting his name.

'Hilde, we have to go inside now.' Maria took me gently by the arm and guided me back.

'But I have to find Karl. Maybe these soldiers know where he is and when he is coming home,' I protested.

'I will ask my husband and his comrades whether they have met others on the way. What is your husband's name and which Brigade did he serve in?' A kind woman came over to where I stood. I now saw some of the soldiers were accompanied by wives and children, all beaming with happiness and hanging on to their husbands and fathers.

'It's alright, Hilde, you go in with Frau Bucker. I will pass all the details on,' Maria volunteered.

Once back inside my apartment, I noticed for the first time in weeks what state the kitchen was in. Ursula was standing on a dirty floor, a piece of bread in her hand and her face and fingers covered with homemade jam. I had not washed the dishes, potato peel was on the floor beneath the sink, dirty nappies in a bucket which should have been in the bathroom. I could not see the surface of the kitchen table it was covered with everything I would usually store carefully in the larder.

Maria entered and stood behind me.

'How long has my kitchen been like this?' I asked nobody in particular.

'It's been going on since you gave birth to your baby, almost three weeks ago. Frau Bucker and I have coped as well as we could. Most of the time I still sleep here to keep an eye on things.'

'Three weeks, I had my baby for three weeks?'

'Yes and you have not even named her yet. Time is running out and you have to register her birth soon. We have spoken to the doctor who has notified the Town Hall Birth Registrar but you have to go there next week.'

'But how can I do it without Karl?'

'Hilde, what would Karl think if he saw you and your home in such a state?' Frau Bucker spoke firmly.

'Where are my other children?' I felt like I had been in a fog, which was slowly lifting.

193

'Klaus and Renate are at school and Karl-Heinz is in the Kindergarten, I took them there this morning,' Maria told me.

'What does the rest of my apartment look like?' But before anybody answered I heard my baby crying, turned on my heels and went to my bedroom. There she was, in her cot, her dummy lying next to her, her little hands balled into fists, like in protest at being ignored by her mother. I picked her up, sat on my bed and cradled her in my arms. I opened my blouse and started to feed her. She looked at me, like she had never seen me before.

'It's alright Erika, Mamma is here,' I said and then I heard the bedroom door close softly.

Chapter 64

It was on a cold December afternoon in 1945. It was already dark outside. There was a knock on the door and I jumped. The children looked up from the kitchen table where they sat drawing pictures with the new crayons Karl-Heinz got for his 5th Birthday a few weeks ago. Karl-Heinz always shared everything with the others, he would rather do without as long as his brother and sisters had something. Whatever it was, whether it was something to play with, or something to eat, he would always be the last one in the line, always stepping back, watching and waiting. He was so like his father in that respect.

There was the knock again, I had not looked out of the window since it got dark and it got dark very early in the Winter. I went into the hall. There was a light on, on the staircase, giving a warm glow to the outside of my front door. I saw a shape of a figure standing there. My heart missed a beat.

'Karl?' I opened the door.

A young soldier stood there, rooted on the spot looking at me.

'Frau Paekel, it is me, Paul.'

All the children had left their chairs and were behind me. 'Mamma is it Pappa?' asked Karl-Heinz.

'Frau Paekel, don't you remember me? I met you at the train station.'

Young Paul, whose mother had entrusted Karl with his care when they were deployed to the Russian Front, ten months ago. I would have not recognised him. He had grown up in the short time and looked much older than he should.

'Is Karl with you?'

He shook his head, standing there, in his uniform, with his field cap in his hands. I took a step back and let him in. He looked at the children still behind me all staring at him.

'Klaus, can you take the others and go back to your drawings.'
Klaus was just going to speak but looked at me and thought better of
it.

I took Paul into the sitting room and closed the door behind us.

'Paul, where is Karl? Do you know when he is coming home?'

It took Paul a while to find his voice. 'We were not far from
Bryansk, we were surrounded by Russian infantry and tanks. We
could hear them coming closer in front of us and heard fighting to
our left and right. We had buried ourselves into a hollow with about
a dozen others. Officer Paekel was still in charge, although we had
already run out of ammunition. Officer Paekel called me over and
told me to hand him my rucksack. He filled it up with all the rations
we still had and told me to put it on. He said he had spotted an
opening to the back of us. Then he instructed me to get up and run.
When I did not move, he pulled me towards him by the collar of my
jacket and shouted.

*'Soldier! This is a direct order. If you disobey you will be court-
martialled. Is that clear? Did you hear me, Soldier? Now you run
and don't look back.'*

'Frau Paekel. Frau Paekel?' I hardly heard Paul. 'Frau Paekel, he
gave me this before I ran. I had to promise him to deliver it without
fail.

He handed me a letter he had taken from his pocket and I
instantly recognised Karl's handwriting.

'My dearest Hilde,

*I write this letter with a heavy heart but in the hope it reaches
you. Getting this letter means that sadly I might not be in a position
to come home. I miss you and love you so much. If I die it will be
with your photo in my pocket close to my heart. Please forgive me if
I have ever hurt you. Please be strong and keep my memory alive by
telling the children about their father who loves and misses them.
There was so much in our lives we wanted to do and see. Please do
it for me and I will be with you every step of the way. Please live
your life and through you and the children I will also live.*

I love you Fraulein Hilde.

Yours always Karl'

Epilogue

Hilde received the official notification of Karl's death several months later. It said Karl had died in action whilst being deployed on the Russian Front.

Maria was now in direct contact with her husband Egon who was in a Prisoner of War Camp in the South of England near a town called Portsmouth. Egon subsequently was released in the summer of 1946 and returned home.

Frau Bucker and Hannelore remained good friends with both Hilde and Maria.

Erika and her husband Erich arrived on Hilde's doorstep in March 1946, having fled in advance of Russia taking over part of Germany. Tilsit, Hilde's family home town was now declared to be Russian.

It took Erika almost a year after the War had ended to get to Hildesheim. After Oleg had managed to arrange all of their escapes just before the end of the War, everybody first had to gather in one of the Refugee Camps outside Berlin. Only German people with proof of relatives in towns throughout the country were processed and allowed to continue their journey.

Hilde's mother, brothers Helmut and Guenter and sister Grete went to live with Lisbet in Limbach-Oberfrona in the German State of Sachsen.

Gisela wanted to go and join her boyfriend in Sondershausen, in the State of Thüringen, east of the Harz Mountains.

Herbert had found a new wife and they went to live in Rostock, near the Baltic Sea.

Arno had not been heard of by the time they all left and Traute stayed with her Russian Officer.

Oleg, Ludmilla and their children wanted to rebuild their lives in Berlin and went in search of Oleg's uncle's old delicatessen shop.

Erika told Hilde, 'If it had not been for Oleg's bravery and resourcefulness, none of us would have made it out of Tilsit.' Erika also confessed having questioned Oleg how he managed to get the right paperwork for himself and his family to get out of Poland to work and live on a German farm in the middle of a War, but he did not tell her.

Hilde decided to fetch the black metal box, the one her mother had sent for Hilde's sixteenth birthday and in which she kept her documents and her memorabilia of precious moments.

Hilde took out the photograph of her dancing with Field Marshal Rommel and told Erika the details of the Night she danced with Rommel.

Hilde and her mother Hildesheim 1937.

Erika and Erich 1944.